Entering the World of the Small Church

Anthony G. Pappas

Foreword by Douglas A. Walrat

D1157160

An Alban Institute Publication

Grateful acknowledgment is made for use of the following:

Excerpt from *Traits of a Healthy Family*, by Dolores Curran. San Francisco: Harper and Row, 1983. Used by permission of author.

Passages from *Return to Laughter*, by Eleanor Smith Bowen. New York: Harper and Row, 1954. Used by permission of author.

Excerpt from "The Ghosts of Our Ancestors," in *Primitive Worlds: People Lost in Time*, by Elman R. Service. Copyright © National Geographic Society, 1973. Used by permission of author.

Excerpt from *Amish Society*, by John A. Hostetler, 3d ed. Baltimore and London: Johns Hopkins University Press, 1980, 285–56. Used by permission.

Passages from "The Folk Society," by Robert Redfield, *American Journal of Sociology* 52, no. 4 (January 1947). Used by permission.

Library of Congress Catalog Card Number 00-104846

ISBN 1-56699-236-2

CONTENTS

99957

S ome things really are better the second time around—like Tony Pappas's *Entering the World of the Small Church*. Whether you are a first-time reader or someone who is opening this book to get reacquainted with an old friend, you are bound to benefit from the insights you will gain. As a wise advisor once said, "It is not how many books you read that matters, but how many times you read the right books." This book is one to read many times.

It's a book I needed and didn't have when I first entered the world of the small church in 1958. I spent the first twenty-five years of my life entirely as a member of large churches, beginning on the west side of Chicago in the 1930s. In seminary I did all my supervised practice in large churches. It seemed totally appropriate to me and my friends when I was invited one summer day in 1958 to serve as the founding pastor of a new suburban church. Later on during the evening of the day I received that invitation, an old friend called to invite me to preach in a small, rural church in upstate New York. No doubt his call was one of those providential coincidences that guide our lives. From the moment I entered the world of the small church, I knew it was to be my world. Except for two brief years (two years, two months, and five days, to be exact) when I served as senior minister of a very large church, I have been engaged in some form of ministry with a small church. Currently in "retirement," I serve as the treasurer of our eighty-member Presbyterian church in western Maine.

I came to the world of the small church as an outsider and had to learn to understand it. Only after many years did I appreciate why people in small churches do what they do the way they do it. In the beginning I often thought the other leaders in that first small church were stubborn when they were slow to change. Only later did I appreciate that those who have always lived with limited resources, and expected always to live with limited resources, are being responsible rather than stubborn when they are slow to change. One lay leader helped to orient me to reality when he said, "If what you propose doesn't work, you will move on; we will always have to live here with what we have." Now, as treasurer of a small church, I really understand what he meant.

As an outsider, I knew I had to learn how to lead in the world of the small church. Later, as a teacher helping others learn how to become leaders in small churches, I discovered that even those who grow up in small churches and small communities have to learn how to be effective leaders in small churches. I used the original version of *Entering the World of the Small Church* as a text in courses on the small church for many years. The first time I taught one of those courses I was surprised to hear how much one of the students had appreciated the course; I knew he had grown up in a small town and a small church. "I have wondered all these weeks why you enrolled," I confessed. "I expect you already knew almost everything we discussed in the course." Not so.

"I have lived almost my entire life in a small church," he told me, "but I never understood it until I took this course." Sometimes all of us need help to understand even what we are most familiar with. Whether you have years of experience with small churches or are new to small churches, you will gain lots of useful insights from Tony Pappas's book.

This book affirms small churches. Small churches are not for everyone. In fact, the notion that "small churches are beautiful" is not now as popular as it was when a book of that title appeared in the mid-1970s. In the final chapter of this book Tony Pappas quotes a church leader who predicted in 1999 that 75 to 80 percent of the churches existing then will be closed by 2050. No doubt many of those he expects to falter are small churches. But this contemporary observer's proclamation seems akin to Mark Twain's comment when he read a copy of his own obituary: "The reports of my recent death are greatly exaggerated." Twenty-five years ago I heard another well-regarded church leader proclaim, "The future belongs to the mega-church!" "Some people's future," I thought at the time, "but not mine." The future he envisioned has arrived—and it includes both mega-churches and small churches.

Affirming small churches probably still seems countercultural to many people. But I think it is more like affirming a minority. Being positive about small churches is no more countercultural than being positive about being black or Native American or rural. Small churches, like ethnic groups and regional groups, are simply different, each one another culture, part of the larger world and also a world of its own. Some people enter and soon leave the world of the small church where I am a member because they can't thrive there. I experienced the same misfit when I became pastor of that large church. I couldn't thrive there and I moved on. That didn't make either me or that church bad. I just didn't fit.

When it comes to churches one size doesn't fit all. The world of the small church is a manageable world for many of us who do not do thrive in the large-church world. The careful work of ecological psychologists like Allan Wicker shows that people who thrive in small congregations are often unable to find either ministries that are possible for them or the sustenance they need to continue as disciples when they are forced by mergers to become part of a large church. When their small church becomes large they either find another small church to join or, sadly, stop participating in church altogether. Those who suggest that "Walmartization" is the inevitable future of the church offer a forecast that seems to me superficial and even insensitive.

The small church is here to stay. It has defied the dire predictors before and will do so again. Tony Pappas's book is a gift to all who care for small churches. Whether you are entering the world of the small church for the first time, or simply trying to understand it better, this book will help you to become a more faithful and effective leader.

DOUGLAS A. WALRATH
Professor Emeritus
Bangor Theological Seminary

I grew up in a small church. Spent every Sunday morning, most Sunday nights, and many Wednesday nights there. Went to church picnics and suppers, youth group, and missionary meetings. Knew everybody and everybody knew me (or at least whom I belonged to), so I couldn't get away with much. Memorized my Bible verse on the way to Sunday School and vowed to follow Jesus anywhere (except overseas). Was glad I was saved (went forward during seven different altar calls till I was sure!)—but sad that my schoolmates from the Congregational Church weren't going to heaven with me. Yep, I grew up in a small church.

For a long while I didn't know there was a small-church world. The town was small and the outlook was small, so my church didn't seem any smaller than anything else. It was just church.

Then I went off to college. This was not applauded by the deacons who firmly believed that thinking was the root of all evil. My parents were very supportive, however, believing that any schooling was preferable to the school of hard knocks in which they were still enrolled. My ticket out lay along the track of education.

In college I was well trained. I learned to think logically and analytically. I learned that the knottiest problems could be chopped up into little pieces (which made it much easier to sweep them under the rug). I learned that all problems have solutions. It took much longer to realize that all solutions have problems. I learned that nothing has to be the way it is; everything can be improved (in other words, nothing is sacred). I learned about the history of progress and the progress of history. I thought I was taking courses, but I learned a way of thinking about life. And I learned that it's easy to get into seminary with a college degree.

At seminary I relearned everything I had learned in college, though now in reference to the church. I learned how to be a professional church leader, how to administer the church, how to organize the coming of God's kingdom, and how to assimilate new members. I learned about the early church and late church members. I learned the theology of a funeral service, and I attended a funeral service for theology. I learned that God is dead (but I thought this was exaggerated). I learned about the church universal and, through the divinely inspired case-study method, the church particular. I learned about churches with get-up-and-go, California churches à go-go, and churches which did not pass go (or collect $200 from every member).

Then I went to my own church and got vertigo. In January 1976, with my bride of a year and a half, I moved to Block Island, Rhode Island. I had been called to become the full-time pastor of the First Baptist Church, a congregation tracing its roots back to 1661, and the same quest for religious freedom that motivated Roger Williams and John Clarke. Block Island, named for Dutch explorer Adrian Block, is ten miles off the southern coast of Rhode Island (I wound up in overseas ministry after all!). At that time it claimed 500 residents, although to qualify for Revenue Sharing—available to communities of 500 or more—the local census takers allegedly had to take a detour through the cemetery. The Harbor Church, nicknamed for its location, gathered about two dozen for business meetings, three dozen for worship services, and four dozen for covered-dish suppers! Into the hands of these folks my wife and I placed ourselves, along with all our earthly possessions (which didn't fill a modestly sized U-Haul), as the ferry steamed away. Never did we have reason to regret our commitment.

Two determinative realities emerged for me in this congregation and in this community. The first was obvious and immediate: We were loved. Maybe this congregation was filled with "lovers." Maybe the congregation had given up on obtaining a full-time, young pastor and so I was perceived as a Godsend. Maybe my wife and I were seen as two lost, little kids—as one parishioner later described us—and we evoked pity. Maybe God went ahead and prepared the way. Whatever the reason, the kindness and genuine concern toward us were palpable: Tea at a parishioner's after that first, violent ferry ride. A deacon dropping by when it started "breezing up" (wind gusts approached 110 mph that day!) to make sure we were "tight." Casseroles, house plants, seed packets—all evidence of country kindness. Pay raises each year, even if modest, meant to say, "You're appreciated."

Parishioners who laughed at my sermonic jokes; others who didn't but would defend to their death my inability to tell them! And always, always the feeling of loyalty, the knowledge that people would be there when you needed them. We were loved.

If love was the first reality, learning was the second. But it emerged more slowly. In fact, I almost missed it. It arose first as confusion, frustration, dissonance, with visible manifestations. For example, the clothes I had so carefully purchased on a seminarian's budget so I would fit in at my suburban congregation during field education hung unused at one end of my closet, while my flannel shirts became threadbare from constant use. But it took me longer to change my mental clothes. I acquired this new attire in unexpected ways.

For example, the church sign. Our building was not easily distinguished as a church building since it is an appropriated Victorian hotel with a sanctuary wing stuck on. It seemed logical to me that to attract new members, as well as visitors, guests, drop-ins, and so forth, we should identify ourselves as a church. The trustees hemmed and hawed and finally decided that holding a church business meeting was necessary to decide. What I thought would be a cut-and-dried vote turned into a raging debate. I held up the "sign side" in a brilliant opening statement but rapidly lost ground, primarily because I couldn't make a lick of sense out of the opposing comments. It was only years later that I realized the logic of the opposition: those who need a sign to know where the church is aren't enough a part of us to be church with us. I understand there is a tombstone, circa 1882, in Hartford, Connecticut, which reads: "Those who cared for him while living will know whose body is buried here. To others it does not matter." So, you see, the situation changes, but the attitude remains the same.

Or consider pledging. Closing the year in the black was always touchy business in our congregation. Our treasurer had devised certain "tricks" to help out; I later realized. One was to withhold certain types of receipts (for instance, bank interest) from reporting. This made our situation appear even worse than it was, but it also motivated the parishioners (including the treasurer herself) to give more! Thus we were, each and every year, near bankruptcy from August to December. But somehow, miraculously, we would finish the year a few dollars to the good. Once I caught on, I questioned this approach. "Wouldn't it be more businesslike, straightforward and dependable to have a pledging system?" I argued to our trustees. "Impossible!" they answered. "Why?" I queried. "Because we are all farmers and fishermen and we never know what kind of year we will have," they answered. "We give as we can." I was too stunned to reply. Yes, parishioners gave as they could, but not one member made a living farming or fishing, not since a hurricane destroyed the entire fishing fleet and most of the barns in 1938!

Or consider mission. In my view, mission is a matter of commitment and discipline. Christ is active in the world, and to the degree of my ability, opportunity, and faithfulness, I support his mission in its totality. Foreign mission and local mission differ in geography but not in essence. One I support through dollars and prayers, the other through blood, sweat and tears. Qualitatively, however, they are the same. It's just that one is close at hand.

But not so for my deacons. Once I raised for their consideration a new denominational mission offering. Their concern was significant, but it was to protect the congregation from this offering! So concerned were they that each deacon pledged individual contributions to prevent a general appeal! To them mission was ministry: local, personal, face-to-face. Resources were limited and small, and stewardship consisted of not wasting the group's effort to care for its own.

So, you see, I had entered the small-church world. But I didn't know it then. I was confused and frustrated, and my initial reaction was to attribute madness or badness to them. In other words, to the degree that these people opposed me and my position, I thought they were lousy Christians, or nuts, or both. Fortunately, a third alternative emerged by God's grace and my parishioners' patience: they were operating out of a different system than I was—a system with different values, perceptions, and understandings. In short, they had a distinct view of the world. The world looked different to small-church people, and their thought processes differed from my abstract, rational, educated, individualized, goal-setting point of view. Their worldview was not right (moral, Christian, biblical) just because they used it, just as it was not wrong just because it differed from mine. If any worldview is to be "righted," however, it must be changed from the inside. And if we are to minister effectively in the small church, we must first step into that world. After all, Jesus stepped into ours.

This book is offered as a first-draft road map of the small-church world. Welcome. But I warn you: as you journey, your perspective of the small-church world will proceed from frustration to quaintness, to satisfaction, to significance, to eternity. In the end you may no longer be interested in becoming an executive minister, district superintendent, stated clerk, bishop, or even president of the Alban Institute!

Acknowledgments

I would like to thank the many friends who have been a part of the process of nurturing this book from an idea dimly perceived to a reality. Thanks to Stan Gaede, professor of sociology at Gordon College, for connecting me with the tools I needed and seeing the promise in my first rendition. Thanks to John Wilson, professor of church history at Pittsburgh Theological Seminary; this is the book you kept telling me I should write. Thanks to Celia Hahn, former editor-in-chief at the Alban Institute, for her contagious enthusiasm. Thanks to Eleanor Long, who must by now have the equivalent of a Ph.D. in cryptology for deciphering my handwriting. Thanks to Sue Purdy for outsmarting our computer; and to the Ohio State Council of Churches, Town and Country Department, which gave me the forum to first test these ideas. And thanks to my wife, Cindy, for her many kinds of support through two editions of this opus; to my children, Rebecca and Jason, whose desire to know how it was coming helped it to be; to the fine people who are the First Baptist Church of Block Island, teachers all; to the fifty congregations of the Old Colony Association of the American Baptist Churches of Massachusetts, who continue my education; and to David Lott, Alban Institute managing editor, whose amazing talent makes commas, content, and concept all work together!

PART ONE

Understanding the Small Church

CHAPTER ONE

Introduction

S mall churches come in all shapes and colors. Sizes, too. God touches, or seeks to touch, every one in a distinct way, each endlessly fascinating, interesting, diverse, and unpredictable. I know. I try to "ride herd" on fifty of them in southeastern Massachusetts (which is like herding cats, as someone described it). After twenty years of pastoring intensely in one small church (the First Baptist Church of Block Island, Rhode Island, and the context of the earlier version of this book), I am now the area minister for the American Baptist Churches of Massachusetts, Old Colony Association. So my focus has shifted from one tree to a little forest.

Although the issues remain remarkably the same—health, survival, ministry, change—each congregation responds and expresses itself in its own special way. Consider some of my churches. (Please excuse the use of "my"; I know all churches are God's, but these particular churches are in my corner of the vineyard!) One church's claim to fame is that its sanctuary is the oldest, still-standing American Baptist church building in the country. But its real mark of distinction is that it has the highest clergy-to-membership ratio of any congregation in the history of the universe—one to one! Here's how it happened.

Over the last two generations the congregation had ebbed steadily until there were less than ten at worship, all elderly. And worship was held only twice a month! When the octogenarian pastor announced his desire to retire, I had no idea how I could find a replacement, even at the current fee of $25 per service! When a pastor who had just moved back into the area to care for her ailing parents asked to candidate there, my prayer was answered. (Baptists do not place pastors; we call pastors upon a congregational vote after a candidating process.) Or so I thought, until a meeting with the current pastor revealed that two Sundays off a month would meet his need to retire! Finally after much prayer, and a little fasting (I lost my appetite at the breakfast meeting), we came up with a plan: the services on the second, fourth, and fifth Sundays of every month would be reinstituted and the new pastor would candidate for those! Two parishioners showed up for the vote and agreed to the plan. In effect, these two members could each claim their own pastor!

One of my favorite places to preach and worship is with an African American congregation of about two dozen members. They are the most enthusiastic of my churches. They "Amen" you and "Hallelujah" you all the way through the sermon. Clearly they are happy to be the Lord's and to be together. But I must confess I was unprepared for some of the ways they express their exuberance. I had always regarded the public reading of Scripture as fairly serious stuff and not in need of human concurrence. So when the congregants jumped to their feet and started cheering and clapping halfway through the Bible reading, I was so stunned I could hardly finish reading. On further reflection, I suppose there may be a few passages worthy of hooting and hollering!

Or consider one of my old, faithful, swamp Yankee congregations. They have been around since the British cried out, "These New Englanders are revolting!" They have by sheer grit survived lean time after lean time. They know how to do that. But they called a pastor with the gift of evangelism, and the number newly coming to faith now nearly equals the number of old-timers. Faced with relative prosperity, this stalwart church is discovering that it is not sure how to deal with good times. So frustrated are the pastor and the old guard with each other that the pastor is taking "his" new members and starting a new church!

Or consider one of my "never say die" churches. To get pastoral leadership, the congregation has had to configure and reconfigure itself: The church has yoked uneasily with another congregation. Members have purchased the leftover time of a staff person from the big city church down the road. They have had numerous student, lay, and retired pastors, but they have kept on keeping on! Last year their pastor challenged them to go through the New Testament in one month, so they ordered audiocassettes for every family. Ninety percent of the families purchased them and listened their way to Revelation! Name me any other church of any size whose membership has that thoroughly immersed themselves in Scripture!

Or consider a certain church founded over a century ago in what was once a primarily white neighborhood. As the members aged, they watched their children move away. They watched their peers die. They watched their neighborhood change as people of a different culture and language moved in. Sensing God's call to renewed ministry in their neighborhood, they tried to start a Hispanic ministry. It failed. They picked themselves up (all eighteen of them!) and tried again, this time linking with two strong Hispanic churches in different parts of the state. Each Hispanic church lent a number of seed families, creating an instant, though temporary, congregation. On this basis other Hispanic families were invited and attracted to come to worship, to faith, and to commitment. Today only one seed family remains; the others have returned home or to other assignments. Nevertheless, this ministry now numbers nearly one hundred, and the once all-white congregation has voted to ratify the Hispanic families as members of their congregation, thus putting their future entirely in Hispanic hands. What trust, what faith, what love!

I could go on and on telling you the stories of success and failure, vision and myopia, health and peculiarity, the past and the future. I could, but you get the idea. Clearly God delights in small churches. Although they wrestle with many of the same internal and external challenges, each one responds differently. Each church is a unique mix of the common and the individual. Each has its own story, its own script, and its own future. Often I am frustrated, even angry, and sometimes despondent over my small churches. But I am never bored!

THE UNIQUE MINISTRY OF SMALL CHURCHES

Small churches have a unique ministry in the twenty-first century. Much of what they have to offer is what they have always had to offer: the incarnation of the living presence of God in real social relationships. But from here on, the way they offer this quality of salvation will need to reflect the changing dynamics of society.

The primary quality of small churches is their relational dimension. Small churches offer family-like connections. God did not create human beings to live alone. Each of us needs a place—a place where we are seen and known and valued. Today's society fosters displacement. People chase their careers through fifty states. They are transferred to the remote parts of the country or world. Children go off to college and are scattered to the four winds. In the face of this atomization, the scale and the nature of small congregations allows each person to be known individually and loved uniquely. Small-church pastor and author David Ray[1] claims that in congregations of up to 125 persons, fellowship occurs spontaneously. People naturally get to know and enjoy each other. But beyond that number fellowship will suffer unless it is organized. Small congregations, then, present the perfect scale for persons to be in natural relationships. The worldview of small churches is unalterably anchored in the personal. We will consider this dynamic in greater depth subsequently.

The second quality of small churches is that every congregant is, or can be, important. Freud summarized the components of a meaningful life as "to love and to work." Love is embodied in the personal dimension of congregational life. Meaningful work, a senses of personal significance, and the opportunity to develop God's creation are also present for each member of a small church, in reality or in potentiality. I don't have a clue how to try to influence a vote in the U.S. Senate, but in a small church I am continuously able to give shape and direction to things. About a dozen church leaders were gathered as part of a quarterly steering committee for one of our newest churches, a Cape Verdean congregation. A young man wandered into the church late but was nevertheless invited to sit at the table with us. He did not contribute anything verbally, but he certainly was paying attention. After the meeting ended the pastor discovered that the young man had thought he was coming to a Bible study. When the pastor apologized for the mix-up, the young man said, "I really enjoyed the discussion, especially on how to get the word out to others. I have a degree in marketing, so if you would like me to help I would be happy to!" The pastor signed him up on the spot. Not only was that young man's talent put to work, but he was soon seen as a Godsend!

The third quality of small churches is their ability to enable spiritual growth in a natural and customized way. In a small church the pastor is not far from any member. Anyone has access to the pastor and spiritual counsel. Often growth and service are delivered through on-the-job training. Apprenticeship, for example, is a natural vehicle for growth in the social structure of the small church. Likewise, there are myriad opportunities for hands-on ministry. Small-church members can get involved in whichever activity is most harmonious with their personal learning style. In a small church each and every gift of the Spirit is of value. Consider the case of a mother who brought her learning-disabled daughter to a large-church Sunday School. The mother thought a large church would have the resources to include a disabled child, but she was asked to remove her child because of the disruption in class. When she tried again, this time at a small church, the members reorganized the class to enfold the child in love. Their small size gave them the flexibility to respond with personalized attention for the child.[2] Certainly there are always plenty of general tasks to do in a small church, but there is also the opportunity to accommodate each person's special style, talent and needs so that each person can grow spiritually in his or her own way.

Finally, when it lives into its divine nature, the small church is a redemptive presence in society. The small church is often dismissed as quaint, old-fashioned, peculiar, filled with "characters," and so on. While those labels are sometimes accurate, they can obscure a more profound truth: the small church is a subversive element in our culture. A healthy small church takes the prophetic stance that bigger is not always better! Powerful things are done in and through small churches for very few dollars. In the small church people matter more than "success." The small church demonstrates a social ecology of stewardship and harmony. People are ends not means.

SIX CHALLENGES FOR SMALL CHURCHES

For these redemptive qualities of the small church to actually permeate society, small churches must find a way to get beyond their current barriers. These barriers constitute six challenges faced by small churches today:

1. *Traditionalism threatens the future of our small churches.* Traditionalism, namely, the attitude that what has been must always be, is the argument for never trying anything new: "We've never done it that way before." For example, even if statistics would show that 90 percent of persons under the age of forty can't stand organ music, small-church folk may think this fact less significant than the fact that "we do organ here"! Of course, there is much good in what has been and much we should preserve. But God also calls us to new things, new places, and new ways. Can we recapture not the behaviors of the past that have led to our present traditions but the pioneering spirit that shaped those behaviors in the first place? If we can, there is hope.

2. *"Niceness" threatens our small churches.* Certainly church members should be nice and polite, you say. How can niceness be a threat?

Granted, being nice is more a goal for some churches than others, but it becomes a threat when being nice is more important than speaking the truth in love. In one congregation a person with bipolar disorder nearly ran the church into the ground. Members focused on being polite lived in terror of his next explosion. Other members dropped out. Community members aware of the problem refused to join. Finally only a handful of cowed, depressed folk were left, all because the congregation was too nice to discipline unacceptable behavior or push him into getting help. Jesus was meek, but he was not always nice. He could assert himself and confront people. When something of eternal value was threatened, he had the chutzpah to speak out. Small churches that don't advocate health now may not have the option tomorrow.

3. *A "club" mentality threatens our small churches.* A club exists for the satisfaction of its membership. The church of Jesus Christ does not! Now, I am not saying that small-church members need to be dissatisfied. But a little holy dissatisfaction wouldn't hurt. We need to remember that the Body of Christ must always be about the business of sharing good news with those not yet within the congregation. Churches that have lost their heart for evangelism are living out their final chapter.

4. *Paralysis in the face of conflict threatens small churches.* Wherever there is life there is conflict. Some conflict is healthy. Indeed, it stretches people's understandings, it motivates them to strive for excellence, it helps them to see greater options, it even saves us from boredom. But conflict that is endemic or extreme will poison and then paralyze a congregation. Christians fall prey to the misunderstanding that disagreements are of the devil. Conflict is resolved neither by denying it nor by avoiding it. Progress is frozen in many small churches because the members have never learned how to fight in a Christlike manner, that is, they haven't learned to speak their truth with love, to strive for win-win outcomes, or to subordinate their positions to God's will. So either the conflict degenerates into destructive patterns or the factions become locked in immovable positions. Neither helps. "Agreeable disagreement" must be learned.

5. *Negative "scripts" threaten small churches.* Some small churches are dying by their own lines, lines such as "We're too small," "Nothing we try ever works," "What's the use?" or "Where are the 'good old days'?" One of my churches closed a few months ago. In the conversation that led to its closure I inquired about recent outreach efforts. The leadership informed me that the congregation had offered a series of public seminars,

but "only one or two new people came." Parishioners told themselves they had failed. I said, "Two people represent 10 percent of your current congregation. If you could have loved them into joining, you would be among the fastest-growing churches in the country!" But their script, not mine, prevailed, and death was the result.

6. *The cost of our buildings is a threat to small churches.* Although many small churches have attractive, serviceable, appropriately located, and fairly well maintained buildings, many do not. One of my churches has a mortgage payment larger than all its other expenses combined. Another will be anteing up around $100,000 to clean up an old oil tank. Many have thirty to forty worshipers strewn about a sanctuary that will seat three to four hundred. One faced repairs so costly that it chose to knock the building down! Our church buildings do have spiritual significance beyond their bricks and boards. But the community of Jesus Christ must not be allowed to degenerate into a building-preservation club. It will lose its spiritual edge and its message of salvation and hope. If the call of God is heard, "Go into a land that I will show you," it needs to be obeyed!

Small churches face a number of challenges as they seek to be faithful in the twenty-first century. They also have a needed message of faithfulness for the days ahead. Will small churches succeed in fulfilling God's will for them? Time will tell, of course, but it seems to me that the greatest single resource to appropriate God's tomorrow is *quality leadership*—leadership that seeks God's heart, leadership that loves the small church, leadership that understands the nature of the small church and can act appropriately within it.

This type of leadership cares about the small church. It believes that each congregation is a magnificent creation of the almighty God and that each congregation is called to a ministry that it alone can accomplish. It believes that each congregation, no matter how small, is a mission outpost in its time and place. And it believes that each congregation has its own wonder and beauty that, by believing in it, can be released.

This type of leadership is committed, to God and to these people, for the long run. One of the worst things to befall the small church is revolving-door leadership, especially pastoral. Pastoring in the small church is not a job, a function to be done until the five o'clock whistle blows. It is a relationship, a covenant, a marriage, if you will. Abrupt or frequent transitions ensure that all available energy will be expended in adjustment and recovery, leaving precious little for mission, evangelism, discipleship, and growth.

Above all, this type of leadership is competent. It knows what a small church is all about. It can maneuver in the small church terrain. This is the leadership we will be describing in the rest of this book.

CHAPTER TWO

A Small-Church Model:
Theory and Theology

The story is told of six blind friends in India. They could scarcely conceal their excitement, for they had heard that an elephant would be brought to their village that day. As they waited along the roadside, they discussed what an elephant must be like, for they had heard much about elephants but never experienced one firsthand. When the kindly elephant owner saw them, he stopped his massive beast and invited the blind men to approach the elephant. The six blind men rushed forward until they made contact with the great animal. The first blind man grabbed the elephant's trunk. "Ah," he said, "an elephant is like a great snake." The second blind man happened upon the tusk of the elephant. "So," he said, "an elephant is like a smooth spear." The third bumped into the elephant's leg and, hugging it for support, concluded, "An elephant is like the trunk of a great tree." The fourth reached up and felt the elephant's ear. "Now I know," he said. "An elephant is like the huge fan Rajahs use to keep cool." The fifth walked into the enormous torso of the animal and reasoned that an elephant is like a fortress wall: broad, tall, and impenetrable. The sixth latched onto the elephant's tail. "Yes," he said, "I can see now why an elephant so impresses everyone. He is like a rope which swings freely, traveling wherever it wills."

Like those of the six blind men, our views of reality are powerful in determining our actions and our satisfactions. Because the world around us is far too complex for us to rediscover it each day, we each have an operational model of reality in our heads. In order to function we act as if the vast world around us is like something we have experienced, and thus stored in our minds as a picture, image, opinion, attitude, or even emotion. We are not always conscious of these operational models. In fact, we seldom are. They come to our awareness when things don't seem to be adding up right, when the world seems to be out of whack. At these points we receive insight about our operational models, and we have the opportunity to change them in light of a greater reality. As the six blind men discovered, models can be "true" as far as they go. But a model is not itself reality. No model is 100 percent accurate. Seminary professor Paul Minear, in his book *Images of the Church in the New Testament*,[1] describes the models used by the New Testament authors to depict the church—all ninety-six of them! Different models have different degrees of helpfulness, though. In the sciences models are thought to be helpful if they are (1) broadly applicable and (2) capable of predicting further facts and relationships. As we think about the church, we should go further. Theological models ought also be (3) true to the biblical revelation and (4) appropriate to real people in specific societies and eras.

HISTORICAL MODELS OF THE CHURCH

The church has always had a tendency to see itself in the image of the predominant social reality of its day. It might not be too bold to say that Augustine saw the holy people of God in light of the power and organization of the Roman Empire. His thinking went a long way toward legitimizing in the minds of Christians that unholy hybrid known as the Holy Roman Empire. Similarly, around 1000 A.D., Aquinas saw his heavenly Lord as like his experience of earthly lords, and so the church was saddled with a feudal and hierarchical ecclesiology for half a millennium.

In contrast to that model, Calvin and the Reformers saw individual election as the primary reality. The social structure was vitally significant but was a derivative from that reality. In this position they articulated theologically what was already happening socially and economically: the ascent of the "burghers." So intimately connected was this theology with the new social structuring that the word "protestant" and the phrase "work ethic" have become one in modern usage.

Today we also tend to understand the church in light of the structures, values, concerns, and ways of operating that characterize the predominant social reality, namely, corporate America. Churches produce a product to meet a need in the marketplace. Those with inferior products—for example, "folksy" sermons, off-key choirs, spotty programming, modest buildings often in disrepair, that is, the small church—go bankrupt and die. This is the proper result of a free enterprise system. Adam Smith's invisible hand strikes down inefficient and archaic small churches, enabling the corporate church to prosper. The corporate church differentiates its product from other brand names, uses long-term planning cycles, employs a marketing strategy, and sees growth as its overall criterion of success. (And, as we have recently seen, it is able to provide its CEO with unbelievable perks, including money, jets, condos, and even sex!)

All such societal images of the church are spiritually suspect. Some have a modicum of truth. Some are satanic. None should be used uncritically. Yet it is our natural tendency to do just that; we have been so steeped in these societal models that they have become second nature to us. Yet the model of the church which we employ will determine, to a large degree, our faithfulness. So it behooves us as Christians to be judicious in our choice of ecclesiastical models.

Two Biblical Models of the Church

There are many, many models of the church and God's people in the Scriptures. But two are particularly helpful to our understanding today because they are such fundamental and rich concepts. The first model depicts the church as "people of God," the second as "Body of Christ."

The Church as "People of God"

The image of the church as "people of God" recurs throughout biblical writings. Deuteronomy 7:6f. provides a most insightful instance: "For you are a people holy to the Lord your God. The Lord your God has chosen you out of all the peoples on the face of the earth to be his people, his treasured possession . . . because the Lord loves you." "People" is not used in this passage in the same way it is used in modern English; it is not a reference to an aggregation of individual human beings. Rather, it is a coherent social entity, an ethnic grouping. In sociological and anthropological jargon it is a "folk society."

The term "folk society" (which will be described further in chapters 3 and 4) was coined by anthropologist Robert Redfield.[2] His idea was to create a spectrum upon which existing societies could be sequenced and compared in a systematic way. At each end of this societal spectrum Redfield posited an "ideal type." At one end he located the type of society of his own experience: Western, urbanized, technologically advanced, highly educated, highly mobile, based on contractual social bonds, and so on. On the opposite end he placed the folk society, an extrapolation of societal characteristics he encountered doing anthropological fieldwork in Central America.

A folk society is composed of a group of people who

1. are small in number,
2. have a long-term association,
3. know each other well, and
4. have a strong sense of belonging.
5. The group is isolated from other groups in neighboring areas and
6. has a high identification with the territory it occupies,
7. often functioning as if it is "in a little world off by itself."
8. Wisdom, prestige, and authority strongly correlate with the age of each individual,
9. enhanced by the fact that each generation goes through a similar sequence of life events.
10. There is a simplicity of roles,
11. a primacy of oral over written communications, and
12. a straightforward level of technology.
13. Position in the folk society determines an individual's rights and duties,
14. behavior is as much expressive as it is effective, and
15. relationships are ends in themselves, not a means of achieving an external object.
16. Social recognition is a greater motivator of behavior than material gain.
17. Qualities that contribute to long-term stability, not change, are valued.
18. Tradition determines actions, and
19. moral worth attaches to the traditional way of doing things.

These specific qualities of a folk society objectify what we might today designate "a tribe," which comes closest to the meaning of the biblical "people." In the Deut. 7:6f. passage above, the biblical author proclaims that God is making for himself a people, a tribe, a society in which his glory and holiness can be reflected. So it is that Peter writes of the church: "You are a chosen race, a royal priesthood, a holy nation, God's own people, that you may declare the wonderful deeds of him who called you out of darkness into his marvelous light. Once you were no people but now you are

God's people" (1 Peter 2:9-10). It is entirely consistent with the Scriptures, then, to picture the church as God's tribe. As such, God's people rightly have their own language and culture, history and traditions, patriarchs and heroes, stories and legends, institutions and ways of doing things. The church is to be a society distinguishable from other societies and one that demands total allegiance and participation.

THE CHURCH AS "BODY OF CHRIST"

The model of the church as "Body of Christ" may at first glance appear to vary significantly from the first model. It may even seem contradictory. In fact, it is complementary. Where the first model takes an external perspective, seeing God's people as an entity, the second looks inward, seeing the internal life and functioning of the church in terms of its parts and their relationships. Paul writes to the church in Rome, "We, though many, are one body in Christ, and individually members one of another. Having gifts that differ according to the grace given to us, let us use them . . . let love be genuine . . . love one another with brotherly affection; outdo one another in showing honor" (Rom. 12:4-10). Here and in the other "Body of Christ" passages in 1 Corinthians and Ephesians, Paul is concerned with the dynamics that are to characterize the internal life of God's people. Love and deference are to be the attitudes with which Christians relate to one another. Mutuality and complementarity are to be the ways Christians live together. Here individuality is a means to enhance the whole church, not an end to itself. The emotion evoked is a family feeling: one is to feel and act toward the church the way one feels and acts toward one's own family.

TWO CURRENT MODELS OF THE CHURCH

THE BUSINESS MODEL

Once, some years ago, I determined that my parish needed to grow, develop, and progress. I went to my local Christian bookstore and came home armed with books from seminary professors, "successful" church pastors (in other words, pastors from large churches), and denominational officials, each explaining in great detail how one can get one's church moving. I learned all about systems theory, mission statements, goal setting, and strategizing. I learned about resource analysis, and writing and managing by objectives. I learned about long-range planning and one-minute managing. I learned about flow charts and force-field analysis.

In the end I learned that the church thinks of itself as a business. In this organizational approach the church is like any other organization: a thing, created by its managers, brought into being by management's decisions and behaviors. The approach is rational: there is a logical connection between behaviors and desired outputs. The approach is structured: the relationships between component parts and the procedures employed to accomplish organizational tasks are determined by the mind of management and explicitly formulated, so much so that these relationships are subject to being captured in an operating manual. The approach is bureaucratic: it works through a hierarchy with clear chains of command and responsibility, and an *orderly* method of accomplishing the task is valued. The approach is task oriented: it exists to get a job done even when that job is fellowship (so churches train deacons to organize and shepherd cell groups). The approach is energy consuming: the organization cannot continue to function at its present level unless it receives massive inputs of resources. These resources are in terms of people, property, time, effort, skills, and dollars. In this business or organizational model the church is thus understood.

I find this business model of the church theologically nauseating. Certainly, any grouping of human beings that exists over time has some form and degree of organization. Thus the organizational approach has some validity. But this model serves only at the lowest level of understanding the church. The church, even the simplest and smallest of churches, has something more than this organizational aspect to its nature. It has, somehow and in some way, the living presence of God within it and upholding it. Such a living aspect must be accounted for.

THE BIOLOGICAL MODEL

I prefer a biological model, a model which reflects that the church is more organism than organization. In the biological model the church is not seen as a thing created by the will of its managers; it is not primarily rational. It is seen as the living Body of Christ (see above) created by the loving intention of the Lord of all life. Of course, its bylaws may be logical and its committee work efficient, but it lives on a much deeper level. It lives on the level of shared experience, tradition, and even habit. Its thinking exists to serve this deeper level of being. This church is not essentially structure; it is essentially process. It is alive. It grows and shares and moves through the events and the flow and the sequence of life.

Yes, the church has a structure, but this structure is a conduit for the truly important elements that flow through it: the loving relationships with one another and with the God who makes them possible. The church is not essentially hierarchical. It has means for accomplishing its tasks, but these means are more personal, more mutual, more habitual. People do much more than hold offices, form committees, and serve on task forces. The church is not primarily task oriented; it is primarily relationally oriented. The church may do a lot, but its real goal is simply to foster togetherness, fellowship, community. The church is more energy neutral, or even energy creating, than it is energy consuming. Large inputs, especially large pastoral inputs, are seldom necessary to assure its continuation or health. The church keeps going, almost with an indescribable inertia, muddling through but enjoying its life.

The biological model is actually not one model but a cluster of models. Let us now consider "family" and "cell" as two prominent biological models.

THE CHURCH AS FAMILY

The family serves as a traditional and very rich model of the church, and the small church in particular, according to Dr. Harold Moore of the Center for Career Development and Ministry in Newton, Massachusetts, who has compared the small church to a family system.[3] Moore sees parallels between different types of small churches and types of families, specifically, the sequences churches and families go through over time and the dynamics within small churches in terms of family systems (for example, the "symptom bearer"). Duncan McIntosh[4] has developed a classification of churches according to family type, which he believes can predict the future growth potential of a particular church: (1) the constricted-family church, which resembles a tightly bound nuclear family and is unlikely to grow over time; (2) the restricted-family church, which resembles a family of siblings and is likely to experience some growth over time, and (3) the reproducing-family church, which resembles an extended family of cousins and is likely to experience high growth over time.

Professor Maynard Hatch, formerly of Central Baptist Seminary, worked with churches in a field-placement setting to measure their "temperature" (degree of health) by using certain characteristics of a healthy family. These characteristics, fifteen in all, are described in Dolores Curran's book, *Traits of a Healthy Family.*[5]

The healthy family

1. communicates and listens
2. affirms and supports one another
3. teaches respect for others
4. develops a sense of trust
5. has a sense of play and humor
6. exhibits a sense of shared responsibility
7. teaches a sense of right and wrong
8. has a strong sense of family in which rituals and traditions abound
9. has a balance of interaction among members
10. has a shared religious core
11. respects the privacy of one another
12. values service to others
13. fosters family table time and conversation
14. shares leisure time
15. admits to and seeks help with problems.

THE CHURCH AS A CELL

A second model within the biological category was developed by Carl Dudley, who sees the small church as a "single cell of caring people."[6] By analogy one can speak of a concentrated nucleus where the hereditary, determinative qualities are located, a broader "sea" in living contact with the whole and a solid but permeable boundary with its greater environment. Because of these living and intense qualities, Dudley speaks of pastoral leadership in the small church as more "lover" than "manager." A living cell is not managed, but must be cared for, nurtured, and respected. It is alive and performs the functions of life naturally and (so far as we know) is without conscious thought. Its DNA gives it shape and identity. Like a cell, a small church is self-bounded, its components live in close proximity, and it tends to replicate its nature over time.

THE "MEDLEY MODELS"

We move next to what I call the "medley models." These are a series of church models that vary according to the size of the church. Arlin J. Rothauge, in his booklet *Sizing Up a Congregation*,[7] classifies churches in four categories: the family church (up to 50 members), the pastoral church (50 to 150), the program church (150 to 350), and the corporation church (350 and up). In *Looking in the Mirror*[8] Lyle Schaller depicts churches according to the average number in worship. If there are fewer than 35, he likens the church to a cat, 35 to 100 to a collie dog, 100 to 175 to a garden, 175 to 225 to a house, 225 to 450 to a mansion, 450 to 700 to a ranch, and more than 700 to a whole nation. These models are interesting for their variety, creativity, and specificity, but they obtain these qualities at the cost of an overall model of the church.

AN ALTERNATIVE MODEL: THE TRIBE

As an alternative to these normative models, I propose that we think of the small church as a particular type of society, namely, the folk society to which we referred earlier. This tribal model allows the combining of the two previously mentioned biblical models with anthropological insights.

This model is thoroughly biblical, not only because it is contained in the Bible, but because it is fundamental to understanding the dynamics of God's action in the Old Testament and the hope of God's people in the New Testament. From the call of Abraham to the heavenly predictions of Revelations, God has been working to actualize exactly this type of society. In this is our biblical origin and our spiritual hope.

A tribal model is also explanatory. From my own experience (although a full description would require another book!), I have come to see that those behaviors, values, and perspectives which so frustrated my rational and goal-oriented approach in my own small church are thoroughly explicable in terms of folk-society life. In fact, they are predictable. This is yet another reason for putting forward a tribal model: it is most helpful in predicting behaviors and responses, and it is a useful guide for discerning a functional, meaningful, and satisfying leadership.

ROLES

Of the many specifics of this tribal approach, the first is the realization that roles, more than offices, determine the social landscape. So much has been made of some of these roles elsewhere that I need do no more than list them here. There are patriarchs and matriarchs, elders, chiefs and shaman, gatekeepers and scapegoats, and the storytellers, as well as the group of gossipers who create the stuff of future stories! The list could be much longer, of course, but what is important is the types of roles, not the rational "official" structuring pastors often think is important.

COMMITMENT

The second realization is that what holds a tribe, and a small church, together is commitment, not a favorable cost-benefit ratio. The social bond is covenant, not contract. Members understand their own well-being in terms of the well-being of the whole, and we are in it for the long run. This covenant is our life. As the little boy explained after carrying his injured sibling up a hill to home, "He ain't heavy, he's my brother."

SOCIAL CONNECTIONS

A third characteristic of tribal society concerns the priority of social connection. A wise businessperson will hire an outside consultant or contract out a job as appropriate. To the businessperson the outsider is not an enemy, per se, but a potentially positive resource to be utilized expeditiously. For a tribe nothing could be further from the truth. To tribal members the outsider is an enemy almost by definition. Not knowing who we are and how we do things puts the outsider beyond the very history and social interaction that give meaning to our tribal world. The outsider is an alien presence, like a pebble in one's shoe, irritating, a deviation from the correct order of the world. How often are first-time, small-church pastors puzzled by the congregation's lack of enthusiasm for their evangelization plans and the frequent outright dismay when they succeed in bringing in new people? Such pastors would be wise to remember that it is not only these new people who are outsiders; even the pastors themselves are initially, at least, outsiders to the ways and mores of their small churches.

The problem of integration is not limited to the tribal model, however. Even in the business model the newcomer is integrated rationally through a "new members class" or socially by placement in a subgroup of the church. In a tribe, by contrast, a newcomer would likely be initiated by listening around the campfire but kept in a marginalized place. After a while the tribe's stories will become the newcomer's stories, the tribe's way of doing and seeing things will become the newcomer's way, and he or she will slowly be incorporated into the tribe. For most small churches today the campfire has been replaced by the covered-dish supper, but the function is the same.

FOCUS

Then there is the issue of focus. Businesses are concerned with any aspect of the environment that will affect their well-being and profitability—new government regulations, prime interest rate, potential shortage of raw materials, shifts in consumer preferences, labor demands, to name a few. With its self-image drawn from the business world, the church likewise has its attention focused on its environment: world missions, Third World relief, social action, denominational politics, demographic patterns, and new member recruitment are the types of things that concern a church. The tribal church, however, cares about certain aspects of its environment, but its main focus is internal. What is going on with those in its social world is the issue of most importance. So the endless prelude to every board meeting—who is in the hospital, who is pregnant, whose cousin dropped in from Oshkosh to visit—often considered wasted time to a goal-oriented pastor, is crucial to those in the tribal church.

Likewise, the attention and action of the business corporation are aimed at keeping its future options open. The corporation tries to position itself in relation to the future. The last thing it wants is to find itself in a dead-end position without options for change. The tribe, on the other hand, does not really care for options. What the tribe desires is continuity. It wants tomorrow to look like yesterday. Life is, in general terms, the way it ought to be. What is important is to live it out, not change it. Jockeying to position oneself among possible future options is a peculiar, if not incomprehensible, exercise. Where we have been is where we want to go. The patterns of our life are a given: God has established them, and we are to live them out.

Each of these characteristics of the folk society has implications for leadership in the small church. Many of these implications run contrary to the prevailing wisdom, the predominant society model. Nevertheless, if the tribal model is more true to the reality of God's church, then it should be our touchstone for faith, understanding, and action as we seek to serve our God in the small church today.

Now let us enter the world of the small church.

PART TWO

An Inside Look at the Small-Church World

CHAPTER THREE

Perceptions in the Small Church

THE RELATION OF THOUGHT AND ACTION IN A SOCIAL SYSTEM

Thought and action. That they go together is obvious. But how? This is not quite so clear. Since even asking the question is a mental exercise, the long-standing presumption is that we think and on that basis we act. We desire something and we exert ourselves to accomplish that end. We envision something new and we expend effort and energy to bring it into being.

While this is so true to our experience that few would deny it, its value has been questioned of late. In fact, the opposite position has gained currency in recent years, namely, that the relationship between thought and action runs more from action to thought than from thought to action. In other words, understanding follows behavior. When people act a certain way they soon come to understand that as the right way to act.

Who is right, those who claim thought leads to action or those who claim action leads to thought? This chicken-and-egg controversy, I submit, is actually a red herring. It is irrelevant whether the chicken or the egg came first. What is important for us to know is that in our experience the one leads to the other in an ongoing sequence of life and productivity. Thought and action are related to each other in a continuous process of cause and effect, of occurrence and response, of event and reaction. So our mental map of the world leads us to action that reinforces or reinterprets our mind's chart, which leads to further action, and so on. The map in our minds is much less a chart to our future than it is a description of our present limitations.

Individuals' thoughts and their group's behavioral norms form a whole.

That is, we tend to act in ways that "fit" with our understanding of the world. And we understand the world in ways that "fit" with the way the world plays out around us as well as our part in that. Over time a congruency develops between one's thought patterns and the behavioral patterns of his or her social world. It is not just that deviation from the standards of the group (such as backbiting) are punished (for example, by confrontation and rebuke). It is that the very way in which one thinks about the world is shaped by the social group of which he or she is a part.

This may seem obvious. And yet it is my experience that this wholeness, this connection between one's thought and one's world, is almost totally overlooked in the current "wisdom" on church renewal. This is particularly a problem for the small church. For those who write (often large-church pastors, seminary professors, and denomination officials) tend to live in a world different from their small-church brothers and sisters. Thus their thoughts on church renewal, faithfulness, and health are foreign to a small-church person. I am certainly not claiming that the small church is, in and of itself, perfect, complete, and faithful. What I am saying is that to understand how we can encourage our small churches to be all that God intended them to be, we need to understand how the small church thinks, how it perceives its world, and how it normally acts within that world. The thought/action system of the small church varies significantly from that of other institutions. We might call the thought patterns of small-church people a "folk mentality." For it is closer to the thinking of people in folk societies than to the thinking of people in complex, bureaucratic, and abstract organizations, as we shall see.

SEEING THE WORLD AS A TOTALITY

DISCRETE LIVES

"TGIF": Thank God It's Friday! So a current expression sums up our attitude toward the workweek and praises the coming of the weekend. For the American worker there are two times, even two worlds, in each week. There is the Monday-through-Friday working week. Time is put in. Money is earned. Maybe, if one is lucky, careers are advanced. Then there is the weekend. For some this is real life. It may be that the gin mill is substituted for the treadmill, but the change is greatly valued.

Leisure is a boom industry in our society. That is where it is at. Some people will come right out and say, "I live for the weekend." On whether this is good or bad, I have my own thoughts. But that for these people—millions in our society—the world is fractured, broken in half, is beyond debate. In fact, for these people it is impossible to speak meaningfully about life as a whole, because it simply is not. Rather, life is composed of a series of discrete lives: work life (8 A.M. to 5 P.M., Monday through Friday), family life (evenings and weekends), church life (Sundays and a few meetings during the week), play life (weekends and vacation time), social life (a few weekend evenings a month, for most of us). These various lives can add up to a busy week, to be sure, but they nevertheless remain separate.

In such an arrangement we do not expect to have any significant level of overlap between "lives." In fact, it can be downright disorienting to have a person from our work life show up in our church or social life. An overlap like that complicates the neatness of the compartmentalized life. Sometimes it is tolerated. Sometimes we act to restore the separation ("Dealing with him all day at work is enough. I am not going to sit next to him at worship, too"). I have one friend who highly values an intense fellowship group he is part of in a large, urban church, yet he never sees any of the other members outside of group meetings.

INTEGRATED LIVES

Contrast the view of the discrete life to the way I learned to live while a pastor at the Harbor Church of Block Island, an island eleven square miles in size off the Rhode Island coast. For the two decades I lived there, I was one of about eight hundred year-round residents. Of those eight hundred, I could place nearly everyone by name or face, or connection. It was not because I was the pastor that I knew nearly everyone. Everyone knows everyone. In fact, I was probably one of the last to know "the latest" because I was often "out of the loop" (I didn't own a CB, nor did I hang around the post office parking lot!). At Harbor Church, when a new person came to worship there was an effort during the subsequent coffee hour to place him or her. The bold introduced themselves to the stranger, and the shy checked with the pastor, "Who's that?" (Note: This desire to avoid a lacuna in the social chart of the parish should not be confused with a welcoming in Christian love. That may or may not have been involved as well!)

Except during the summer season, I would go through a typical day without encountering anyone I didn't already know. The cast of characters in my work, leisure, social, and other lives varied only slightly. So that world may have had different facets, but it was essentially a unity, a totality. Some may have considered this confining and limiting—as in some ways it was—but I considered it a structure for growth. For in this kind of world I was unable to run away from my interpersonal difficulties.

Some years ago my stance on a school issue offended a teacher and his wife. Their response was to snub me in public. Being a sensitive soul, it hurt to have my "hello" or friendly wave returned with a glare or a quickly turned head. But because I could not avoid running into them in the course of daily life, I had to figure out what to do. I was determined to live by my standards, not their response. So I continued to be friendly, sometimes exaggeratedly so. I seemed to cope better if I made it a game. Nevertheless, after a while came a nod, and then a mumbled "hi." When sickness struck, I went to visit and was received. Afterward they resumed coming to church. Over the course of the illness my visits were received with genuine warmth. In the end I was asked to conduct the funeral service. My tears were sincere and my efforts were appreciated by the spouse. I grew up because I had nowhere to run, except away from my own immaturity. This world is a totality.

Life is unitary and global. Its movements constitute a oneness. Such wholeness is inherently satisfying and feels right and normal. Gaps and breaks in one's knowledge of the whole are problematic, motivating people to "fill in the gaps." This enterprise is a (maybe the) major "work" of small-church people, frequently to the consternation of the pastor whose sights are set on bringing in God's kingdom. Those present at the deacons' board or the governing committee often seem to be engaged in a conspiracy to avoid the pastor's programmatic agenda. Who's sick? Who's pregnant? Who's going to and returning from college? Who's facing moving to a nursing home? These questions constitute the basic agenda of small-church people. The answers plug the holes, they fill in the gaps. They make the world whole again. Now, Pastor, was there anything on your mind?

The Unity of Time

Life is unitary in the sense of time, too. The routine of life is daily, not weekly. The week divides into weekdays and weekends more on the calendar than in experience. A while back, again at Harbor Church, I was assisting an engineer in testing the water table on a lot my wife and I hoped to build our "dream" house (that is, our own home) on some day. The engineer was working at an amazing rate. "Why?" I asked. His boss had said that this was his last job for the week. He smelled a long weekend and so he was hurrying to get back to where he could enjoy himself. His behavior made me think about my fellow islanders. Little new or different happens on the weekend there. Most residents are self-employed. There are no clocks to be punched. Work to be done hangs over their heads twenty-four hours a day, seven days a week. Fishermen launch out according to the weather, not the day of the week. During the summer islanders work seven days a week. In the off season work schedules wind down or gear up. In the twenty years I pastored there, I never established a regular, viable day off, not because I wasn't interested in one but because the parishioners didn't comprehend why one would take a day off from (not work, but) life. Life has its ebbs and flows, daily and annual. They reflect the very flow of nature. They are natural and integrated. They form a whole.

No Need to Reinvent the Wheel

Life in the small church is also understood as a totality because it doesn't change much over time. Life is recurrent: it is a sequence of issues, circumstances, and requirements that are essentially repetitious. Once in place a behavioral response, though arbitrary, becomes a true solution. It is a true solution in that it meets or at least addresses the problem and, therefore, liberates one to think about other things in life, or to be at peace. Life is not able to be totally resolved. Bringing into question a behavioral pattern (a solution), no matter how irrational that pattern seems from an outside perspective or has become due to the changes caused by the passage of time, is frequently perceived as a disruption in our familiar world.

The following story illustrates this hypothesis (I only changed the names to protect the innocent). "Okay," Suzie began, "now that we have agreed that each of you wants to teach the same Sunday School class as last year, let's turn our attention to Sunday School rooms—which class should meet in which room." Suzie was the new wife of Bill Prescott, who grew up in Poplar Knolls Community Church, was missed while away at the state agricultural college, and is now back home, running his dad's farm and resuming his place in the life of his church. Suzie was welcomed as a new member of the church family. After a year of teaching Sunday School she was invited to chair the Christian Education Committee and she accepted, much to the relief of the aged incumbent who had long felt as though she had done her turn and it was time for younger blood to take over. "I've tried to figure this out," Suzie continued. "The larger classes should meet in the larger rooms, and—"

"Except that the largest class isn't the largest class," chimed in Allan, long-term teacher of the rambunctious fourth, fifth, and sixth graders. "The largest class in enrollment is the senior highs, but if two or three come it's a banner Sunday. My class is third largest in enrollment, but we get a bigger turnout and we need a lot of space."

"Plus the kids associate their class areas—you were sweet to call them rooms, dear—with age levels. My kids look forward to moving into the rear of the sanctuary as a sign of growing up," said Phyllis, a veteran of decades in the Sunday School. "Just ask your husband."

"No matter what we do, one class ends up in the kitchen and another in the entryway," Bob added. "There's no way around it. I gave this a lot of thought when I first found out I'd be teaching where each latecomer lets in the cold air when he or she opens the door to come in. But over the years I've kind of gotten used to it. And frequently I've turned it to my advantage. Snow melting off boots and umbrellas set to dry make good illustrations, you know." Suzie respected Bob. He would never even consider that a half-full cup was half empty, too. "What else you got for us tonight, Suzie? No sense spending any more time on what we can't improve on, anyhow."

"Sunday School classes in same room as last year," Suzie wrote in her notebook. She had stopped wondering why no one else took notes and lately she had begun wondering why she did.

CUSTOM, CONSECRATION, AND CRISIS

As Suzie was slowly learning, in a fixed, imperfect world it is a waste of time to reconsider the origin and rationale of present behavior. Oftentimes this behavior already represents the best possible solution, if only because it is familiar and comfortable. Sometimes, though, the way we do things becomes the right, the morally right, way to do things. Whether our method is logical, rational, appropriate, efficient, or effective is not the question. The way we do certain things becomes part of the fixed order of our universe. To change these things is not viewed as a movement toward greater efficiency or reasonableness, no matter how much the pastor says it is. To change what is sacred is seen as a movement toward disruption, disorientation, and confusion.

If Suzie had pushed to reassign Sunday School classrooms, the teachers might have lived with it, grumbling all the way. But when the pastor proposes that the Sunday morning worship service be moved from 11 A.M. to 8 A.M. because half the people in town have only Sunday as a family day (implication: we don't want church to interrupt the family) and no one milks cows anymore (the purported reason for the eleven o'clock worship hour), small-church people don't respond by counting cows and kids. They respond first by panicking about the spiritual commitment of the pastor ("He's not really saying that he wants more consecutive hours of leisure, is he? If he is only that committed, how can he challenge us?"). Or they respond by questioning the moral legitimacy of this group called the "family" ("The church is family, too, Pastor"). Or they respond by citing their own faithfulness ("Why should we who have sacrificed for our Lord lo these many years change our time of worship to accommodate those whose commitment to follow Christ is that low?").

The eleven o'clock hour on Sunday morning is not simply a functional time. It may have been once, but now it has become a sacred hour. Tampering with it is tantamount to tampering with the Ten Commandments. To either attempt we respond with shock, moral indignation, and if persistent, outrage. So, too, do the elements of worship, frequency and manner of communion, maintenance and use of the church building, and use of benevolences go beyond tradition to sacredness. No attempt to change them on our part can go unchallenged. One of my parishioners says, "If I am unable to worship on Sunday, the day isn't the same. In fact, the whole week seems confused." Worship is for her a point of orientation.

A landmark in the flow of time. Being in God's house, in God's presence, is a sure and certain thing. For many of us it gives clarity and firmness to our time, our efforts, even our very selves.

Whether all of what is sacred to us is sacred to God is open to question. But that it is sacred to us is fundamental. The way of organizing life with which we have become familiar orients our soul. Any change in that method or structure threatens what we hold most dear—ourselves. (Jesus presupposes that we have heart, mind, and soul so that we can give them to God in love.) Any inside attempt at change is seen as perverse, iconoclastic, and disloyal ("We thought you were one of us, Pastor"). Change from the outside, while just as threatening, can be dealt with more readily. Although it threatens, it does not represent the debilitating threat that comes from "one of ours." Rather, external threat motivates self-preservation. It energizes the small church to put aside quarrels, to lock step, to beat back the challenge.

That the small-church mentality can better cope with external threats than internal threat leads readily to an understanding of certain phenomena. If, for example, the pastor is seen as the source of the threat, he or she will be moved to the outside, treated as a foreigner, made to feel the monolithic side of the congregation. For in this external position his or her threat can be better handled. If the threat is not personal but due to circumstance—for example, the church roof blows off in a storm—this threat to the valued order of things will, sometimes almost spontaneously, produce a surge of congregational and community resources. The initial response is, of course, to restore the past, to get things back to the way they were when life felt right. So the roof is repaired and prayer proffered. But should this fail, the crisis reaches a dangerous yet potentially beneficial point. Dangerous because if no resolution occurs, disintegration, debilitating grief, and death may very well result. (The roof stays unfixed and all of the accouterments of worshiping God suffer damage.) Potentially beneficial because it offers a deeper spiritual reality. The God behind our sacred cows becomes more clearly seen. God's calling for a new day may be found. (We convene in the few dry pews to seek God's will and help. Now new options become a godsend!)

The moral for the pastor is simple. If you bring change regarding that which is considered sacred by your small-church people, make sure you locate the origin of the disruptive behavior in the external hand of God. Do not become a prophet crying in the wilderness, for that is surely where you will end up!

HABITS

Small-church people (all people in a folk society, actually) do not like to waste time reinventing the wheel. So most of what is done, or at least the way in which it is done, is done out of habit. Small-church behavior is habitual. It is done more on the basis of experience than thought. A physiologist might say that the locus of direction for habitual actions is the medulla, not the cerebrum. For years, almost beyond counting, Harbor Church has run a fund-raising chicken barbecue every August. The barbecue pit, picnic tables, and the serving stations are all set up in the backyard of the church. A few hundred people who are already familiar with the church situation find their way to the back and enjoy a good meal. For about ten years I tried to persuade the chairman that the pit and table should be set up in the front yard of the church abutting the busiest street in town where passers-by would smell the chicken and see the festivities, and newcomers would decide to participate. Our diners would double in number and so would our "take." Logical, rational, efficient, profitable—you bet. Was it ever done? Not to this day! The procedures for cooking and serving chicken in the backyard were well established. My call to rethink it all was too much to handle! Small-church people are habitual people.

Habits are hard to establish and unlikely to arise out of conscious decision. Instead they seem somehow to occur spontaneously in the midst of the ongoing life of the congregation. No individual can be thanked or blamed. "It's just the way we do things around here." You probably won't believe the following incident actually happened, but it did. Honest. I remember it clearly. Clayton was in his late seventies, but he came to worship regularly (in fact, the only worship he missed was when he had been in the hospital). He kept track, too. A number of times he went more than a hundred continuous Sundays without missing a service! Clayton was the one who handed out the bulletins every Sunday. How he ended up with that particular ministry is lost in the mists of time, but he was dependable and faithful at it. When the deacons decided that the bulletins should be handed out by the ushers as they were seating people—a wise strategy for busy summer Sundays—Clayton was asked to relinquish the bulletins. He refused. The next Sunday two people handed out bulletins, one who did so by rationally delegated authority and the other who did so by custom and habit. Visitors couldn't figure out why they needed two identical bulletins. Parishioners, however (and this reflects the mutuality and interwovenness of corporate habitual behavior), preferred to get their bulletins from Clayton and share a word about the Red Sox or recent activity down at the dock. The following Sunday habit won out and Clayton was restored to his rightful place as the one and only bulletin passer-outer.

Trying to create a new habit (for example, ushers being responsible for the bulletins) may seem like more trouble than it's worth. This fact has undoubtedly caused more frustration to more small-church pastors than any other small-church dynamic. Yet there is a good side to such resistance, believe it or not. The first benefit is that habits are a solution of sorts. Clayton was a good bulletin minister. He came early, he didn't miss anyone, he greeted everyone with a smile and many with cheery small talk, and he was there every Sunday. His slowness and his "country" style were, in retrospect, a small price to pay for such a faithful minister. The second benefit is, as hard as habits are to establish, they are even harder to break! A good habit once in place in a small church can yield decades of benefits. This will not likely occur in mid-sized and large churches or rationally structured organizations that do not live out of enacted memory.

Years and years ago a parishioner at Harbor Church asked me if we could pray together on Saturday mornings. Thus the Men's Prayer Breakfast came into being, sort of. For months, despite repeated invitations to others, he and I were the only ones present. Finally two others joined us. Then, one by one, men of the church and the community began attending. It grew to between eight and twelve men who met every week. Each accepted rotating host responsibilities, they called and transported one another, they shared and prayed and solved the world's problems. The quality of sharing, caring, fellowship, and support was beyond anything a pastor could construct. The Saturday morning Men's Prayer Breakfast is now a twenty-year habit. It took a long time to establish in the minds and hearts (and medulla) of the men, but now that it is there to stay, nothing can stop it. That's a good thing, for it is a habit that has done a heavenly lot of good.

Good such as the Mary D Fund. Mary D., our state nurse, had told one of our breakfasters that in her rounds she was saddened to learn that a number of elderly people were not entitled to benefits because they were a few dollars over the annual income cap for the programs she administered. When the Saturday morning group learned of the situation, a spontaneous collection yielded $41 and the idea for a fund administered in confidence by Mary D. to help our needy neighbors became a reality. By nightfall a man who had been moved by Mary's plea and encouraged by the response of the men's breakfast had finished a number of calls to solicit monies. In one day the fund had swelled to $1,441! Over the last decade Mary has distributed to our neighbors tens of thousands of dollars for fuel oil, food, electricity, medicines, and other necessities, while church offerings, concerts, and anonymous donations have helped to replenish the Mary D Fund.

Good such as advocacy. When the Block Island power company wanted to raise its rates (then the highest in the continental U.S.), it was a big topic of conversation at our Saturday breakfast. Concern was expressed over the accounting setup of the company and the impact the higher rates would have on the poor and those with fixed incomes. It was noted that the Public Utilities Commission was holding a hearing that morning. We scattered from the breakfast, our feelings expressed, but with no plan of action. Concern welled up in my heart, though, and I decided to attend the hearing. I watched amazed as one by one the men of the breakfast joined me at the hearing. We spoke our peace and, if memory serves, we were the only members of the public present. Did that one hearing result in the changed attitude of the commission toward granting rate increases? I doubt it, but it played a small but vital part in the overall movement.

Good such as Operation Outreach, our churchwide building-renovation drive. Over the five-year period of the drive, each time our drive chairman periodically shared his concern with the other breakfasters, encouragement, direction, energy, financial contributions, and even elbow grease poured forth. Today the drive is complete, the building refurbished and up to code.

Yes, the Men's Prayer Breakfast is an old habit, but it's a good habit!

CHAPTER FOUR

Motivation in the Small Church

THE QUESTION OF "WHY?"

A sking why constitutes an interesting window into the way people think. Not only the content but the form of the answer reveals significant structures in one's mental world.

I can still remember when my youngest child was in the "Why?" stage. Everything he observed, every statement of mine was greeted with the single syllable "Why?" Foolishly, thinking this to be a question of substance, I would answer him, as simply as possible. No matter how obvious the content of my response, it was invariably greeted with another "Why?" This continued until my patience wore thin, whereupon the interchange reached its finale with an exasperated "Because!" This was great fun for little Jason, I suppose for two reasons. First, his little mind was starting to grasp the connectedness of life. Things can exist not only in physical connection but also in logical, sequential, and causal relationship. It must have been exciting for him to begin the process of working that through. Second, his questioning connected him to me. The whole interchange became a game in which his relationship to me was explored and tested. Asking why was a way of charting his world.

"Why?" asked of an upper-level manager or bureaucrat is answered in terms of goals. Whatever the behavior of the organization—stock offerings, public questionnaires, new advertising campaign, expanding product research and development, unveiling a new corporate logo, making a political contribution—it is explainable in terms of means toward a specified end. (Even if actions are taken because "that's the way we do things around here," this would never be articulated to a superior or the public at large.

Some rationale would defend the behavior in terms of goal attainment. Habit is not an acceptable reason for behavior.) Asking why becomes a rational exercise in causality. Mission statements, goals, objectives, and strategies are all connected to each other by "why" (going in one direction on the flow chart) and "how" (going in the other). The "why" reveals the logic behind a rationally structured organization.

Ask a small-church person "Why?" however, and an entirely different response will ensue. The first and most likely response will be confusion. Not only is the question difficult to answer, the reason for asking it is almost beyond comprehension. Small-church society is not primarily self-reflective. Self-analysis, asking why about behavior, is not an ordinary activity. The answer is so obvious as to remove the need for the question. The behavior is its own rationale. "We do this because we do this." What we do and how we do it are almost never at issue because we do what we have always done, and we do it as we have always done it. To ask why is almost to question the integrity of the group, to shake the foundations that hold us up. We may have forgotten why we started doing it this way, but now it's our way of doing things, our way of enacting and living out life. So the first response to "Why?" is confusion and, if pushed, defensiveness.

If the "Why?" question is answered (and it seems to me that it is more frequently answered in the small church when not asked), the response takes a peculiar form, usually the form of a story about a spiritual forebear. My Harbor Church congregation celebrated a peculiar institution called "Roll Call." I had never even heard of this practice before assuming the pastorate there (I have since learned that it was a popular custom decades back and is still practiced by a few churches here and there). What was it? I needed to know.

On "Roll Call" Sunday, mysteriously the Sunday closest to October 23, the entire membership list was called out during worship. Fewer than one in four was present, I thought, so why did we recite names of people long uninterested in the parish, of people who moved to California decades ago, of people who may have been dead for years? I couldn't figure it out. Of those parishioners who answered, three out of four simply said, "Here," or some version thereof. The more articulate called out, "Present," the more folksy, "Uh-huh" or "Ayya." A few who were hard of hearing said nothing, but the stage whispers of their pew mates indicated their presence to all. (Why any of these responses was necessary was unclear to me, since any fool could tell who was there and who wasn't.) The final quarter of the quarter shared a Scripture verse or a brief thought. Ah, I reasoned, we wade through it all to get these nuggets of truth. It almost redeemed the practice, until the next year when I heard the same verses from the same people, as if it was their theme verse, learned in Sunday School or given at baptism, designating them forever like a second name. Why, I still wondered.

Two days after "Roll Call" Sunday the church erupted in a bustle of activity. Cooked turkeys showed up. Carvers, table setters, squash peelers—all were working as if choreographed. Within hours a few hundred people were seated and fed, and things were cleaned up. I was impressed, but still mystified. Then I noticed that our treasurer sat at a small table by the front door and collected donations from everyone entering. These she duly recorded on a lined, yellow sheet of paper (she was a schoolteacher). As the cleanup crew finished she whispered to me, "It looks good. We did real well tonight." "Oh, great," I whispered back, carefully guarding our little secret. Later I received a letter from a shut-in member expressing her sorrow for not being present at roll call to renew her faith in Jesus Christ. Was that what was going on? Or were we simply trying to balance the budget, using turkey instead of tithing? My "whys" going unheeded, I finally stumbled on the combination. I asked our treasurer, "When did we start observing Roll Call?"

"Oh, that was back in 1900 when Dr. Roberts was pastor," she answered. "The furnace broke down and he wanted to raise $300 to fix it before winter set in. Since the church was founded on October 23, 1765, he selected the Sunday closest to that date, called it 'Roll Call' Sunday, said he was going to call the membership roll, and asked the church members to renew their commitment to Christ and his church by saving and giving. He got his money and we've been doing it ever since."

Why? Why did we call the roll a century later? Because we needed spiritual recommitment? Undoubtedly we did, but that didn't explain it. Because we needed the money? Undoubtedly, but that was only part of it. We did it because we'd done it. We did it because Dr. Roberts started it. We called the roll because that is what we did. Whether it was logical or illogical, appropriate or not, helpful or not, more or less missed the point. We did it because we did it. Because Dr. Roberts was our pastor and we continued to be his people.

THE PERSONAL WORLD OF SMALL-CHURCH EXPERIENCE

The small-church world is above all a personal world. According to Robert Redfield, "A 'person' may be defined as that social object which I feel to respond to situations as I do, with all the sentiments and interests which I feel to be my own; a person is myself in another form, his qualities and values are inherent within him, and his significance for me is not merely one of utility. A 'thing,' on the other hand, is a social object which has no claim upon my sympathies, which responds to me, as I conceive it, mechanically; its value for me exists in so far as it serves my end. In the folk society all human beings admitted to the society are treated as persons; one does not deal impersonally ('thing-fashion') with any other participant in the little world of that society."[1]

The significant reality in small-church society, the reality that motivates behavior and organizes life, as profit is to business and knowledge is to science, is not things or ideas. It is not even people per se. It is the relationships between people. Of course, individual people are necessary if interpersonal relations are to occur, but individualism is not the significant reality of the small church. How we are connected and placed in a personal world, the movements within our social world, how we are rooted and placed among whom we think of as "us"—this is the focus of small-church concern. This is the small-church world.

This world, personal and relational by nature, is really "out there." But it is also "in here." It is inside the perceptions, minds, and hearts of small-church people. What small-church people really want is to live together, to receive the enjoyment that comes from being a part of this particular social arrangement. Now, in order to live together, one must also live. Building a home, tending a garden, and working a job are also part of life, and a very important part at that. But the people in one's life are not seen as instruments toward the end of accomplishing these goals. Rather, these activities are seen as helpful in maintaining our life together.

One could speak about the goal of life in mainstream American culture as the imprinting of one's ego on one's environment. Thus millions are motivated to build up their world (their business, their career, their bank accounts, their net worth) as a testament to their superiority. It is not enough to be financially successful. One's self-worth must be demonstrably confirmed by relative material success. Other people then become instruments of one's self-interest (for example, employees, business and political contacts, technical resource providers) or the background against which one's achievements are made obvious. One's world is seen as material to organize toward a goal and people are understood as instruments of this quest. The essentially personal small-church relation is a logical antithesis to this extreme statement of the mainstream position. The world of small-church people looks different. Their main goal is not to be achieved. It is a given: the preexistent world of social roles, relationships, and intercourse of which they are a part by nature. Although in reality the behavior of small-church people over time will maintain, modify, or erode that social world, it is nevertheless perceived as something essentially beyond their power to transform. Furthermore people and relationships are seldom perceived as means of achieving a separate goal, but rather as what life is all about.

I experienced this dynamic existentially while a pastor at Harbor Church. At one point my wife had achieved a measure of success with a small business she ran on the island. So we went from barely having two nickels to rub together to being people deemed "worthwhile" sales targets by insurance agents. We indulged ourselves in such luxuries as paving our driveway, taking a vacation to Barbados, and buying an investment property. We transformed from two young kids with stars in our eyes and water behind our ears to adults with investment decisions to make and taxes to pay. We had arrived. We were successful. And we were conflicted. Not morally, for honesty and stewardship characterized both the income and the outgo of our finances. Not morally, but socially. Our neighbors made cracks about our driveway. "Looks like the suburbs," they would say. We were cut to the quick. "Where are you going this year?" they wondered. So defensive did I become that I came up with excuses to justify the demonstration of our success (Barbados was the cheapest vacation package we could find; the driveway was less expensive than what we were paying each year for grading; the property was sold to someone else, but when the deal fell through we just stumbled on to it). At the time, year-round residents on Block Island were the fourth poorest in the state. Initially we were one with them in economic marginality. Later our financial success strained our social world. We felt embarrassed at achieving a modest measure of material surplus. We felt awkward where we once felt completely at home. One day one of our church members solved this problem. He won the state lottery. With his winnings he threw a chicken barbecue for the whole island. With the monies left over he started a scholarship fund. Needless to say, he was still a central figure in the life and heart of the community.

That "success" should be antithetical to one's social world is only problematic to people who perceive the world personally. Small-church people understand the world as ultimately composed of people and relationships. We see the world as ultimately personal, too. Since what we value is the personal, we see the personal in all that we value. Everything reminds us of people. "Which way is she blowing today?" fishermen ask about the wind as they decide whether to take their boats out, boats to which they always refer as "she" or "her," never "it."

The trustees had organized their annual foray into the bowels of the church, otherwise known as "cleanup day." I grabbed hold of a board hidden in the darkest corner and pulled it out under the dangling light bulb to get a good look. It was dusty and moldy with faded and chipped paint, but "First Baptist Church" could just be discerned. Just as I was about to suggest chopping it up for firewood, one of the ladies present remarked, "Oh, look. That's the sign my grandfather painted. There's his initials. This hung over the front door for many a year. Here, let me set it down in a safe place." And she took it from me. An old sign? Firewood? Nope. That was as much her grandfather as if it had been his bones. That old piece of wood reminded her of him, his role in the church, the church as it had been, her childhood, and her life in the church. It was precious. And it continues to survive every cleanup day. Things are not just things. They are connections to loved ones. They are symbols of our social world. They are physical evidences of people, left to remind us of who we are: their descendants, the ones to whom they have passed the torch.

PROGRESS IN A PEOPLE WORLD

The worldview of small-church people is built of people and relationships. But how do they move in this world? What is the underlying thought and logic? To the uninitiated (that is, suburban-raised, seminary-trained, rational pragmatists) small-church thinking is patently illogical. It yields no satisfactory sense. But this is to look at it from an external perspective. When viewed internally it is consistent and even has its own logic. I like to think of the small-church approach as being more psychological than logical. In other words, the question in the small church is never, as it is in business, What is the most efficient means of accomplishing the goal that management has selected? Logically a business firm would marshal cash and financing, experts and skills, data and strategies. It would all be very rational and successful. But in the small church virtually all of these tools are nonexistent. Extra cash is hard to come by, debt financing is often taboo, there are no experts, skills are well hidden, there is no data other than personal feelings, and strategies are simply traditional, familiar routines. The only thing left to the small church is people. So the question in the small church is never simply logical. It is always psychological (internal) and sociological (external). Who really wants to do this? And how can others be motivated to help, or at least not hinder?

Through many years of experience, sometimes thrilling, sometimes bitter, I came to know pretty well who in my parish would take upon themselves the ministry of inertia. "If God wanted us to fly, he'd have given us wings." (Actually, such a ministry can be positive if it weeds out the bad ideas before they become habits.) And I came to know who would take upon themselves the ministry of improving things. (Pastors, beware of these people, too. They can poop you out faster than the inertial can frustrate you!) In truth, some of our inertial people would also exert enormous amounts of energy in improving what we already did. But to do something new or different would be beyond their support, if not their comprehension. I also came to know who would fight an improvement tooth and nail yet become proud as peacocks after the improvement had become our regular way of doing things. So things proceeded in our small-church world, not according to a logical progression, but like a river meandering through a valley, skirting rock outcroppings, looking for the "way of the possible."

CHAPTER FIVE

Problem Solving
in the Small Church

Problems confront every group of people. The small church is no exception. It is the manner in which problems are recognized and responded to that characterizes the small church.

DISSONANCE

In all groups problems are recognized as dissonance, a discrepancy between the way things are and the way they ought to be. In a rationally structured organization, problems occur when the present state of things differs significantly from the goals of the organization. If the rate of return of stock holdings in corporation Z is half that of a savings account at a local bank and one quarter of the return predicted by management, a problem exists. If the new, twenty-two-room Christian education wing was scheduled to be paid off in five years but actual pledges indicate a twenty-year payoff schedule, a problem exists.

In a socially structured organization, such as a small church, problems are also registered as dissonance, but not dissonance with the goals of the organization, for this organization has no goals. (I exaggerate. A small church does have goals, but the are frequently below the level of awareness and often have more to do with continuity than with change. Continuity goals may be survival, congruity of behavior, resurrecting the "good old days," and so on.) Rather, dissonance is recognized when it occurs between the present state of things and how they used to be (when they were right). Problem registration, then, is neither objective nor subject to quantitative indices (except in very broad terms). It is subjective, a feeling that things aren't right, a loss of congruency, a mismatch between experience and memory. "Pastor, those Sunday School attendance comparisons you were sharing with us last month didn't register at all with me. But when I went to take my turn in the nursery Sunday and there wasn't one child for me to watch, it hit me. Why, I remember when it took three of us just to change the diapers and keep the bottles filled! That's the way it should be, Pastor. What can we do?"

IGNORING PROBLEMS

Once registered, problems may be handled by ignoring them. This is not uncommon in small churches and is sometimes a viable response! During my first year as pastor of Harbor Church, the trustees virtually went broke having our old, oversized building repainted. "We must prepare for this in the future," I pleaded, "for we know that paint only lasts four or five years. Let us be good stewards and plan ahead by annually budgeting 25 percent of the last painting bill." I was eloquent in my efforts to protect my flock from the twin dangers of bankruptcy and "unpaintedness." The trustees were not visibly moved, but voted to allocate a certain amount each year for painting, "as the pastor said," in order to get on to the next item of the agenda. I breathed a sigh of relief. In my first year there, I had saved the church. I didn't expect a medal, but I did expect the money to be set aside. I got neither. Each year more pressing bills came up and the painting reserve was spent. Month by month I saw the sword of Damocles growing larger over our heads. The paint began to blister, peel, crack, and chalk before my very eyes. Meanwhile a young man had moved into town and joined our church. He was an independent contractor, which meant he worked on his own schedule doing odd jobs. The trustees asked him if he painted. "Sure do," he replied. What would he charge to do the church? He gave a number slightly over minimum wage. "When can you start?" the trustees asked in one voice. Miraculously reaching windows six feet beyond his fully extended ladder, he finished the job for a fraction of its previous cost. "Not to worry, Pastor. The Lord will provide. He always has. I've seen it plenty of times before. When you don't know what to do, let it go. Something will come up. Just you wait and see."

It may be the problem-solving procedure of an ostrich. Or it may be the way Christ's faithful have solved their problems through the centuries.

Come to think of it, what is budgeting compared to believing? Yet this is not faith abstracted and unrealistic ("I've seen it plenty of times before"). It is a faith born of experience. Somehow the Lord has provided. Maybe it is this sense of the unpredictable happening when needed most that gets folk people through. When the wilderness got too barren, manna and quail appeared. When the drought looked as though it would swallow every living thing, the heavens opened and a rich harvest was reaped. When my parish's island forbears had farmed and fished to the limit of their ability and still found themselves short, some way or another a storm-driven ship stocked with lumber, coal, foodstuffs, or cloth would crash onto their rock shores and provide for their needs. It would have been unthinkable to plan for it. Nevertheless, when it came hearts were raised to God in gratitude ("No sense troubling yourself, Pastor. God will provide").

PROBLEM-SOLVING BEHAVIORS

Sometimes problems are not ignored. Instead specific attempts to deal with them are made. The types of behavior exhibited in problem-solving efforts can be divided into two general categories. These two categories, or approaches, reflect two different ways of thinking, understanding life, and operating in a social world. The first category may be labeled cognitive, analytical, rational, functional, or organizational. The second may be labeled intuitive, holistic, creative, expressive, or social. The specific label we choose is much less important than the realization that the first category is the one taught and valued in our dominant culture, and the latter is the one usually operational in the small church.

THE COGNITIVE APPROACH

The cognitive problem-solving approach is objective and predicated on increased understanding. It is based on certain assumptions. The first is that behavior proceeds from intention. A second assumption is that the issues of life can be stopped, that the problem can be frozen and considered in its essence and at one's leisure. A third assumption is that the problem-causing elements and the relevant facts are accessible and comprehensible.

A typical sequence of the cognitive approach is as follows:[1]

1. The problem area is frozen and one specific problem is focused upon.
2. This problem is clearly defined (quantitatively, if possible).
3. Its causes, implications, and ramifications are analyzed. What forces created the problem, keep it in place, and resist actual or potential solution efforts?
4. Potential solutions are listed. These must be described specifically, objectively, recognizably, and measurably.
5. The solution state to be achieved is chosen, along with the criteria used for the selection process.
6. An action plan is devised. It must contain specific goals, objectives, and strategies, including performance and time criteria.
7. The action plan is implemented.
8. The problem is solved after a solution has been effected and stabilized.

As an illustration, let's go through these steps with a sample problem.

1. Within a seven-day period, three parishioners complain to you, the trustee chair, that the sanctuary is dirty.
2. After an extensive interview with each of the three, you determine that the problem boils down to the following:
    a. All three have had dust and grime on their clothing after worship, when their clothes were clean before sitting on the pews.
    b. Dust in the pipes, it is alleged, has accumulated to the point that it is the cause of the asthmatic hum in the organ.
    c. Dust on the communion table is so thick that the pastor could (and did!) write with his finger, "What hath God rot?" (All three deemed this message almost as bad a problem as the dust!)
3. You decide that this problem, its causes, and its (potential) cures need further analysis, so you distribute a questionnaire to the congregation following worship the next Sunday. The computer-tabulated results indicate that thirty-one out of thirty-two adults present and voting thought the sanctuary could be cleaner. (Incidentally, the other vote, a write-in which read, "the sanctuary is perfectly clean and has been for years," came from Mildred, who for the last ten years has received $4 a week to clean the entire church building. She has quit her cleaning position over the "questionnaire outrage" and is now threatening to quit the church. The pastor wants to know why you couldn't have bought her a new dust rag and given her a bit of encouragement instead of "making a big stink.")

4. You determine that the solution states are as follows:
   a. No cleaning. When the church gets filthy someone will notice and spontaneously and graciously clean up.
   b. Apologize to Mildred.
   c. Raise the cleaning budget to $30 a week and hire a Felix Unger type. (Take the additional $26 out of the pastor's salary.)
5. You select solution state 4b: "Apologize to Mildred." After all, she is your wife.
6. The action plan: Today speak to Mildred. Tomorrow buy new dust mitt. The next day Mildred resumes cleaning.
7. You carry out the plan, except that the store was out of dust mitts ("has been for twelve years"), so you substitute an old hanky.
8. Problem solved. You monitor the solution by observing all the rear ends of parishioners in line after worship.

THE INTUITIVE APPROACH

The intuitive problem-solving approach diverges widely from the analytical approach and is predicated upon a different mind-set. It is subjective and is not necessarily dependent on rational comprehension. It, too, is based on certain assumptions, these antithetical to those in the cognitive approach.

The first assumption is that intention isn't enough for behavioral change. One of my deacons struggled on and off with her smoking habit until finally she resolved to quit. Eventually she did.

"How did you do it?" I asked her.

"I didn't do it at all," she answered, "God did."

"Well, how did God quit?" I asked.

"I knew I needed to quit. I knew that no matter how much I intended to quit, I couldn't. So I started praying for God to remove all desire to smoke from me. It took six months, but he did it. I didn't have to force myself at all."

In the realm of habitual behavior there is no direct connection between intention and behavioral change. Intention is not irrelevant (for my deacon it provided the occasion for the Holy Spirit's work), but it does not lead directly to behavioral change. (This is a good place to note the object of behavioral change. In the rationally structured organization intentionality leads to behaviors that accomplish a programmatic goal. In the socially structured organization behavioral changes are directed at a "way of life" and are thus more difficult to achieve and, if achieved, longer lived.)

Unlike the second assumption of the analytical approach, that time can be stopped and analyzed, in the intuitive approach time is not stoppable. It goes merrily along. It is organic, ongoing, alive. Understandings and actions are accomplished on the run. It is harder to hit a moving target, but small-church people would say those are the only targets there are. The third (and related) assumption of the analytical model, that problem-causing elements are distinct from the problem solving, is patently untrue in the small church. Pogo's aphorism, "We have met the enemy and he is us," is closer to being true. One thing is for certain: when we meet a problem in the small church we realize how "married" to it we are!

If we were to analyze this intuitive approach, it would flow along these lines:

1. *Dissonance arises.* An individual or group becomes aware of a conflict between what is actually occurring and what used to occur. Such dissonance is intuitive and generalized. It is a gut feeling and is focused on an "area," not on a quantitatively specified problem statement.

2. *The problem is "cooked."* The small-church problem solver realizes that all behaviors are interconnected, that one life is part of a whole, and that any change in the established patterns of behavior will be tough to accomplish. Therefore, there is no desire to "rush into things." There is no specific solution state, for the full implications of new, integrated behavior patterns are usually beyond specification, if not comprehension. Instead a general feeling of how things "ought to be" emerges in the problem solver. Frequently this is little more than a desire to return to the way things were before the discrepancy was noted. Because the way to do this is never clear, the problem is put on the back burner to simmer. When done verbally the result is akin to gossip. When done neurally it resembles a scanning process, usually unconscious to those engaged in it. The past is sifted. Sensitivity to "clues" in the present is heightened. Behavioral clones are toyed with. (These actions look and feel like "the way we do things" but differ slightly in the direction of a solution.) Heretofore overlooked connections are made.

"Cooking" may seem a peculiar way to solve a problem, but it is the way most problems are solved. I believe. A rational frontal attack on a problem seldom nourishes all the solution elements possible in an intuitive, subjective, subconscious approach. It is not just that problems are solved "on the run"; it is also that "the run" is the solution!

3. *The "Aha!" occurs.* At some point in the cooking process, if a solution is to emerge, a new connection is made. The problem is seen in a new light, which illumines the direction for a solution. The connection of a disparate element is sensed. A way to get something done that fits like an old shoe emerges. "Of course" is the typical response. "The solution was staring me in the face"; "it was on the tip of my tongue"; "it was as plain as the nose on my face"; "I almost missed the forest for the trees." All of a sudden the solution clicks into place. "Aha!"

   A dramatic example is seen in the conversion of the apostle Paul. His struggle against Christianity frequently "boiled over" into violence against the followers of the Prince of Peace. The spiritual wrestling that had consumed his life for months ended in one brilliant moment of clarity when he realized that Jesus was Lord and all he had been doing was railing against reality! In that instant it all fell into place. The problem of spiritual acceptance was granted (not through his efforts, but) in Christ's grace. Paul's life also demonstrates two further points of the intuitive problem-solving process: first, that "Aha!" leads to evangelism; second, that the conviction of this newfound truth is beyond the need for proof in the social world.

4. *"Aha!" leads to evangelism.* When the connection is made in this manner the solution cannot be contained. If the solution is a sermon, it has to be preached; if a work of art, it has to be painted or sculpted; if an insight, it has to be written or spoken; if a ministry, it has to be enacted. A solution is not complete until it works itself out in expression and actuality. It is not a private solution; it is a gift to the public body. Others must be told.

5. *Conviction emerges.* The truth of the solution is evident in the "Aha!" It does not require, nor is it subject to, testing in the social world. (Just as with the apostle Paul, my faith in Jesus Christ is not dependent upon any particular event in my experience. If bad things happen to me, I do not feel that God was an illusion, unable to protect me from evil. Rather, I ask for strength to survive and grow. I ask what good may come of this, what am I to learn because of this. Everything that happens to me is tested by my faith in Jesus. My faith is not tested by what happens to me.) The solution is prior to subsequent experience. The former

conditions the latter. (This may in part explain why it is frequently so frustrating to a rationally structured person to argue with one whom has a small-church outlook. Logic and reason carry little weight. Conviction born of experience is all there is.)

Again, let us see how these steps work out in regard to the dirty sanctuary problem explored earlier.

1. Within a seven-day period, three parishioners complain to you, the trustee chair, that the sanctuary is dirty. You think about their complaints and recall that last Sunday the communion table was dusty, the organ did sound a bit rheumy, and half of the chandelier bulbs were burned out. You remember when, as a boy, you had to take your boots off on the top step to keep from trudging any dirt into the clean sanctuary. You remember when cleanliness was an obsessive idea, the concept of an immaculately clean church, spotless before the throne of God. You remember what a shock it was when you found out that "the immaculate conception" meant something entirely different to Catholics.

2. That the complaints of uncleanliness are justified is unfortunate. It would have been so much easier to say, "Well, we'll see what can be done," in lieu of doing anything. But the parishioners are right. It is dirty. It is also unfair to blame Mildred, however. She's had to take a full-time job. She has all she can do to cook for you and the kids and keep your house clean. The church just gets a light once-over. After all, she only gets $4 a week—the same amount she's gotten for years. Besides, she only took it on because Rev. Parsons asked her to. He was going to organize a group of families to clean once a week on a rotating basis—another good idea we never quite got around to implementing. Too bad. It was a simple idea that could have been fun for families, and it would have saved $4 a week! (Of course, Mildred gives the money back, so it wouldn't mean any more money into the plate, but it would look like less out, anyhow! And wasn't Mildred just talking to you last week about turning the job over to someone if she could only figure out whom?) Well, now, that rotating idea isn't bad. One family a week would work out to only once a quarter.

3. What if each ushering family came in an hour early—they usually do anyhow—and vacuumed and dusted? It would be like our service to God. We would each have a part in keeping God's house clean. Then,

instead of complaining, we could put our energy to good use. What an idea!

4. You decide to call an emergency meeting of the trustees an hour before church this Sunday. We'll go over the whole idea and work any bugs out.

5. Now people will be proud to usher folks into the pews they've just polished!

Summary

Problems in the small church are registered and solved differently. They are registered as deviations from an ideal past. Problems are felt, solutions are mulled. Particular behaviors are less a part of a viable solution than is forming new habits, finding integrated patterns of behavior that "fit" and feel right. Rationality and intentionality play a subordinate role. People, their relations and behaviors, their interests and egos, their histories and turf, constitute both the building blocks of a solution and the obstacles to a solution. That is what makes problem solving in the small church so interesting and exhausting!

CHAPTER SIX

Parameters of the Small-Church Mentality

UNDERSTANDING OF TIME

I have always had trouble managing time (exceeded only by my terror at missing an obligation or a deadline!). I figured, if I was meant to be on time, God would have given me a wristwatch. So when I got one for my birthday, I decided, Enough bungling around! It's time I got organized. I enrolled in a time-management seminar and I attended, although I arrived late. The leader had twenty-one Tinker Toys that locked into each other. He called these the building blocks of our seven-day week: morning, afternoon, and evening. He said professional clergy persons should be spending twelve to sixteen time blocks per week on ministry (that's two to three blocks a day, six days a week or so). Piece of cake, I thought. For family time three blocks a week should do it, a couple of blocks for personal time, and whatever is left for painting the house, balancing the checkbook, and cleaning the basement. (I spend almost a block a week in the bathroom, but I couldn't see how to work this in.) I left the seminar that afternoon (having invested two time blocks) tired but inspired. Soon I would be organized.

I worked hard at allocating my blocks. But apparently my emotional block and my parish block (not to mention my "island Block"), were greater than my time blocks. I watched as people burst in on my sermon-preparation block to ask for marriage counseling. I saw my sleeping block fade into consciousness as I stood by a parish family in the wee hours of the morning watching their home burn to the ground. I watched as my visitation block slipped away as, one after another, people stopped me outside the post office to confer about problems they were facing. I despaired of getting anything done. People in this parish just didn't work in blocks.

For small-church and small-town people time is not blockable. In fact, it is not even chronological. Sure, we have watches and calendars, but they are mostly used to tell us where we thought we were going to be rather than where we actually are. Something like the "You are here" spot on the floor maps at the museum. For us time is not a uniform quantity like lumber which can be cut to fit. Time is simply the context within which the significant events of our lives occur. When it ain't blowing a gale and the cod are running, the fishermen are gone. When I go to visit Aunt Gladys, she can't imagine that I have three other people to see that afternoon. She thinks she is the only one. And I better think it, too. If worship runs long and, in a dither, I apologize to the deacons afterward, they look at me astonished. "Well, the sermon was good, the music was great, and a lot of important things were said during sharing time. It didn't feel long. Don't worry about it, Pastor." Time is what's happening, not what the clock ticks.

So is time experienced in the small church. But where is it leading? In our dominant American society time is linear. It is going somewhere. History and technology are moving. If you're not gaining ground, you're losing ground. Nothing stands still. Change is inevitable. Progress is what it is all about. "Every day, in every way, I am getting better." That history has a linear component is evident to small-church people as well as the rest of society. Small-church people know what year their church was founded, and some of the circumstances at that time; ups and downs of their church over the years; when pastors succeeded other pastors; and when each building improvement was made. But small-church people also recognize the cyclical nature of time. For small-church people the course of history is not so much directional as it is repetitive. Just as the seasons follow each other in an ordered sequence, so, too, the seasons of the affairs of humankind follow each other in a dependable sequence. Boom follows bust; neither lean nor fat years are forever; fashions come and go and come round again; each succeeding generation makes the same mistakes its parents made. Nothing is new under the sun.

I brought a lot of energy to the early years of my pastorate at Harbor Church. I organized and helped start new programs left and right. We began a vacation Bible school, an ecumenical choir, a church fair, a Bible study program, and on and on. As a young pastor fresh out of seminary, I was proud of what we were doing. I was pleased with the new direction our church was taking. Our new initiatives were exciting and gratifying to me. And most people appreciated this "new life" in the church. Most, but not all. One particular individual had a standard, and to me frustrating, re-sponse to every new idea I proposed. "So you want to do 'Y'? Well, that's nothing new. Why, when Pastor X was here we used to . . ." (followed by a glowing account of a past program of the same type, but much superior to what I had in mind).

In my own mind I was the young, new, brilliant pastor proposing ener-getic, new, brilliant programs to my flock. In her mind, young, new, brilliant things did not exist. There was nothing new under the sun, only variations on themes of the past. But it was by recalling the past that she was able to integrate and accept my ideas. What I heard as "Big deal!" was really her way of saying "OK. I've seen that before and it's OK. We're still here, aren't we?" At that time, and that level of maturity, I was motivated by linear time (progress) and debilitated by cyclical time (repetition). She was the opposite. Cyclical time freed her to accept the vicissitude of the day.

Lately I have come around to her way of thinking. Time (history, progress) is not a vector shot out into infinity; it is a pendulum whose ex-cesses are righted by its return swing. I find hope and consolation in this perception and so, I believe, do most of my small-church brothers and sisters.

At Harbor Church time was marked by events. What was happening had happened before. And, the first time it happened was the best. I put a lot of time and effort into sermons, committee meetings, and Bible studies, trying to motivate my parish the way I was motivated: to see God's kingdom come to earth, to look forward to God's new heaven and new earth, to look boldly into the future God was preparing for us. It excited me to envision a better tomorrow and it energized me to work for it. But it didn't seem to do much for my parishioners. Most of the folk seemed to be enervated, not energized, by my aspirations. They got tired just listening to my hopes for the future. I began to wonder what was going on. I wondered what was wrong with them.

In order to find out I decided I'd hush up a bit and listen to what they were saying. I heard things like: "Amy? She doesn't get out much anymore, and it hurts her not to be able to help out at roll call. I remember as a kid seeing her work in the church kitchen all day long—morning till night—getting the food ready. But she can't now, so I guess I'm one of the ones to pick up the slack"; and "When Dr. Roberts was here the building was really cared for. If a repair was needed he'd go up and down Main Street till he'd raised the money. Then the men of the church rolled up their sleeves and did it"; and "When Rev. Pratt was in the hospital after that hit-and-run accident, the deacons did the whole service. For weeks on end they preached, prayed—the whole thing, A to Z. So I don't see why we can't pinch-hit when you're away, Pastor." Slowly it began to dawn on me that I was going about this all wrong. I was using the wrong image. It was the Garden of Eden, not the New Jerusalem, that inspired them. It was the "good old days," not a "bright new tomorrow," that motivated them. I was heading in the wrong direction. They were energized, not to create a new future, but to restore the good of the past. Yesterday, not tomorrow, attracted their interest and concern.

This realization made a profound difference in my ministry then, and ever since. I became a history buff. The oral and written history of our church, I snatched up whenever I could. I structured ways in which our history could be explored, shared, and reexperienced. As pastor, I felt free to call us to live up to our heritage. Whether we do so live is open to debate, but that people were listening is beyond question. I had fun rummaging around the attic of our church's memory discovering spiritual treasures. For small-church people time goes the "wrong" way, away from what is new and better. It goes toward the good that was, or was thought to be.

Understanding of Space

Harbor Church's head trustee and I went up to talk to the state fire marshal. Before he'd answer our questions, he had a few of his own. "What is the square footage of your building?" Neither of us knew. "Well, how big is your sanctuary—what are its dimensions?" "Not sure exactly," we answered, "but in the summer 120 fit in without being crowded and in the winter sixty can spread out without getting lost." He wasn't sure that was very helpful. I thought it was great. It met our needs exactly. "How about Fellowship Hall?" he wanted to know. "That I know," I said. "It is exactly one folding table, set with a chair at each end, wide and exactly six folding tables, fully set, long." It was just big enough to accommodate a Sunday School class at one end and the coffee-hour hostess setting up at the other, without disturbing each other. And the food cooperative that distributed from Fellowship Hall had just the right amount of space, as long as they did the pet food outside. And it was plenty big enough for the Scouts' meetings, our annual Christmas party, and our choir to dress for worship. However, it was a bit small for our VBS closing program, refreshments following, and our Christmas Eve present distribution. "That's nice," he said, "but why don't you come back with measurements and a floor plan!"

Once when a wedding ceremony took me to New York I indulged a long-deferred desire and sneaked up to Cooperstown to visit the Baseball Hall of Fame. I wandered around and just soaked up the whole place: plaques on the wall with the faces and stories of the greats of baseball. In my mind flashed instant replays of those I'd seen in action and imaginative re-creations of those from before my time. The belated honor paid to the greats of the Negro leagues, the exploits of those whose names were lost in the mists of time, the contributions of those who made the game into today's national pastime—truly I felt a sense of awe.

Maybe nothing so dramatic occurred when I wandered around my church. But I was never there alone. On the hymn board I would see the numbers handwritten by Stan Pratt. The baptistry curtain, fresh and clean, reminded me of the struggle it took to replace the tattered old one. The organ reminded me of the faithful and creative services of Carrie for almost two decades, as did the walls painted a few years back by Wilbur and the chandeliers cleaned by John, a parishioner who didn't much care for heights. I would notice the chair where Clayton sat getting ready to hand out the bulletins. And each pew was almost shaped to the posteriors of its occupants every Sunday for year after year.

In Fellowship Hall was the flea market that Brad oversaw and the table that the Scouts "wounded." Eileen picked out the floor tiles—pretty but hard to keep clean—and David painted the walls because he got tired of looking at plaster chips. In the foyer hung a picture of Nathan Mott, who built the building a century ago. Only our oldest members remembered him. Steve, who was Jewish but worshiped with us occasionally, sent his painting crew down to give the walls their fresh look. And there was the light fixture which Charlie fought so long and hard to get replaced, forever hanging as a monument to his (and our) failure and the nature of the small church! If I looked closely at the inside of the front door I could still see certain scratches from the day I forgot my dog inside and went merrily along home. Speaking of dogs, there was always a small rug beneath the fourth pew near the wall in the sanctuary for Ina, Duffy's seeing-eye dog. He came to church regularly and yawned during my sermons. Bea Dodge used to bring her dog to worship, too. If he didn't care for my sermons, he just fell asleep at her feet. She died not too long after he did.

The church building, you see, is more than a physical space to gather in. It is a hall of memories. It brings to mind those who have been important to us, to Christ's church and God's work in this place. It is sacred, not only because it is the house of God, but also because it houses the memory of those who are significant to us, those who kept and keep the church going, those who have given shape to the church building as well as our lives, those who have been the incarnation of God's love and care. So space in the small church can never be dealt with only quantitatively. It has a personal, and therefore sacred, dimension.

THE CONCEPT OF CHANGE

I am a convert to the small-church view of the world. I was raised to view the world abstractly, analytically, and objectively. Gradually has my mind been transformed to utilize and value a folk mentality. Sometimes my unregenerate worldview seeps through, however. One such occasion occurred after Harbor Church acquired a word processor. It was given by a church member to facilitate the publication of a parish newsletter. I was thrilled with my new toy. I experimented with it, worked the bugs out, and utilized it to "go to press" more quickly and easily than before. And, foolishly, I wrote an article in our parish newsletter explaining that we were now "on line," that only one in a hundred churches in our land had a computer, and that, therefore, we were on the cutting edge of ministry, in the vanguard of tomorrow. Superlatives flowed like water, for I was proud of our little church.

The parishioners weren't so sure. It struck them the other way. "If ninety-nine out of every one hundred churches get by fine without one of those fancy machines, why do we need it, Pastor?" I should have known better. I was a small-church pastor, after all. I had written and spoken to various small-church groups and I had edited a small-church newsletter before. It was important to me to change the world for the better, but I differed from my small-church people. They did not desire to be in the vanguard of anything. To them "progress" was working the bugs out of our present ways of doing things. It was not important to them to leave their impression on the world, for they had already "impressed" the world that is vital to them: the social world in which they live and move and breathe. What my parishioners really wanted to do was live out the existing patterns of life and enjoy them to the full. Their goal was maintenance, not transformation. Their motivation was to preserve—preserve the existing patterns of behavior, preserve the existing rhythms of life, preserve the feeling of all being right in their world. (Not that all was right. As it is in most small towns, there were plenty of wrongs in their world, as the delight in gossip attested, but these were the "right" wrongs, typical human foibles. "Wrong," or evil, wrongs were those things that disrupted the integration of their thought-action world.)

That behavior is more directed at preservation than transformation in the small-church world is reinforced by the perception that the environment is essentially fixed and unchangeable. One's personal life and, maybe, one's family life may be subject to transformation by personal initiative, but one's potency decreases rapidly as one moves beyond the self. The physical, political, economic, and even social environment are not considered material for the enterprise of change. They are givens. The attempt to change the given order of things is seen as futile, a waste of time. Change itself comes to be viewed negatively. Changes are disruptions and so are negative in form; and changes are so often negative in content, too. A flood, a diagnosis of cancer, an economic depression—all reinforce the concept that the environment is beyond one's control and that the best that can be hoped for is no change at all. Talk aimed at changing things, then, is often unintelligible. Things are not ours to change. But often it is more than unintelligible: it can be debilitating. For people who must bear the unbearable, the thought that their situation is neither their doing nor subject to their correction is somehow liberating and strengthening. It is easier to face fate than our own failures.

In her moving book *Return to Laughter*[1] Elenore Bowen speaks of finding the capacity to keep going, a discovery she made in the African bush tribe she studied and came to admire.

> In an environment in which tragedy is genuine and frequent, laughter is essential to sanity. . . . These people were not individually callous; they were weather-beaten by their constant exposure to disease and famine. . . . The chief's daughter would reject the cripple. . . . The cripple looked into the mirror of scorn held up for him by the chief's daughter and saw himself through her eyes. The cripple's song cursed the witches who had made him so and mocked himself for exposing himself to mockery. Then with his own eyes he looked at himself and found something better than

her picture and worse than his hopes. "Thus it is," his song ended, "and what can one do?" These people had developed none of the sciences or arts of civilization. They had not learned to change that which is, to wish for a better life so greatly that they would stake the familiar good that might be lost with the familiar evil. They were not, as we are, greedy for the future. We concern ourselves with the reality of what is, because we wish to direct change wisely, hoping thus to preserve the good on which we are agreed while yet attaining what we believe should be. They did not seek to learn thus purposely. If they knew a grim reality, it was because their fate rubbed it into their very souls.

The goal of small-church behavior, then, is maintenance, not transformation; preservation, not change. The small-church world is essentially fixed and unchangeable. When change does occur it is often disruptive and harmful and so gives a negative feeling to the very concept of change. And if things are difficult, to add to the burden of endurance, the burden of responsibility for change is often crushing, not liberating.

With these attitudes and perceptions, change, progress, and improvement seem to be virtually impossible in the small church. (As one small-church pastor fresh out of seminary put it, "Get me out of here. I didn't become a pastor to be a chaplain to the status quo.") Is the small church static to the point of being stagnant? Must it be so? Must leadership be nothing but hand holding because the world is unmovable?

How is change understood in the small church? First, change is understood in terms of a state or condition, not a set of activities or programs. Suppose a large-church pastor were asked to document a claim that his or her parish had improved its mission. Increases in mission giving or a litany of new mission programs would be presented. No one would argue or fail to be impressed. To the same question a small-church person might respond, "Well, I don't know. We just seem to be more mission-minded lately. I think it goes back to the time the Native American girl our ladies group had supported for years worshiped with us on her way to college. The sincerity in her voice as she said "thanks" just made us all feel so good. Ever since it just seemed that mission was not just something outside of us that we should be doing, but a real part of us."

The second aspect of change in the small church is that the world is seen as neither static nor in flux; it is seen as moving in a sequence of predictable patterns. These patterns can be specified and so may be seen as static to an outside observer, but they feel dynamic from within. So the ebb and flow of these patterns are seen to be more permanent than individual life and living them out constitutes our individual journey. This may seem an abstract formulation, but it is incarnated in small-church life. This hit me one day as I tried to solve a problem for the ladies' group at Harbor Church.

When I first arrived there was an active ladies group, the Sunday School Builders, or SSB for short. The SSB had fifteen to twenty members at every bimonthly meeting and were very active in the church. Their average age, though, was well over seventy. As one year turned into another, the Lord started calling our SSB ladies home. After some years they were down to half a dozen members, met half as often, and were noticeably less active in church. I started worrying. The SSB had meant so much to the church, we couldn't just let them die out. But how to beef them up? Elect a young president? Push for new people to join? Get them to do "exciting" things? After one meeting I asked my wife for a report. "Well," she said, "the older ladies just seem to like to talk about old times. And that leaves the younger ones not knowing what to do." Finally I asked the most straight-forward SSBer how things were going with the group. Her answer floored me. "Well," she said, "I don't know why the younger women are coming. It is not meant for them. When I first came to the island, the older ladies had their group, the EMRO Society, you know. They are all gone now. We younger ladies started the SSB to help build up the Sunday School for the kids. We were the young mothers of the church then; now we're grand-mothers! But we've had a good time for forty-five years. Soon we'll all be gone. Why don't the younger ladies start their own group?" In the SSB change was seen as the birth, life, and death of the group. The idea of changing the nature of the group so that it would live forever was unnatural and unsatisfying.

This leads to the third aspect of change in the small-church world. Change is understood as growth, development, the fulfilling of potential, the working out of all the bugs. Small-church people do not live for change, but they do change as they live. "What's new?" can honestly be answered most of the time with a "not much." Small-church people go through transi-tions and transformations over time. In general they are not greedy for these changes. They aren't overly interested in the latest popular book, nor do they tend to chase after the most vibrant sharing group. Rather, they see spiritual growth as unfolding naturally, a process tied to the very sequence of life. "When I was a child, I thought as a child" writes the apostle Paul. "But when I became a man, I put away childish things."

Some possible touchstones of this life sequence include dependency (birth to nineteen years), energy (twenty to thirty-nine years), maturity (forty to fifty-nine years), and "generativity" (sixty and older). One is not likely to jump the steps as one might skip a grade. Nor can one accelerate the process any more than one could add a cubit to one's height by thinking. One could jump off the track, through alcoholism or choosing a life of crime, for example, or one could suspend progress by making immature decisions or living an unvirtuous life. We can make decisions that frustrate our growth, but we don't grow by chasing after it. Spiritual growth is, after all, God's free and gracious gift. A virtuous life (honesty, hard work, Christian faithfulness, dependability, constancy, compassion, charity) is evidence both of one's being on track and of openness to life's next step. Development is understood as an unfolding of the patterns of life. Both a folk-society mentality and a rational mentality utilize the concept of journey to describe changes and progress. The rational mentality sees this movement as a journey into the unknown. The folk mentality, however, understands this as movement along a predefined path.

In the folk mentality goal attainment is not a rational, volitional, existential exercise. The patterned changes are well within the very essence of life and are occasioned by being open to life. Yet we do make decisions. Life without points of decision making cannot be considered complete. How does the folk mentality deal with this contradiction? It does so, I believe, by stylizing, ritualizing, and institutionalizing the existential decision. The decision for spiritual birth has its own methodology (for example, sinners' bench and altar calls), language (for example, "born again"), music (for example, "Just As I Am"), and rituals (for example, immersion). It is almost as if all existential decisions have been collapsed into this one so that we can go about the business of life without further disruption. Compare this resolution to well-educated, rational, sophisticated, guilt-ridden suburbanites who know themselves in the quest for existential authenticity. For these people to decide is to live. To change is to be. Ministry approaches that are effective will vary widely between these two mentalities.

THE CONCEPT OF "FIT"

Is it impossible, then, in such a world to do anything new, to make any change for the better, to do something other than what our forefathers did? The answer lies between a definite yes and a debilitating no. I believe that a wise small-church leader (maybe some pastors, too) can nurture behaviors that constitute forward movement toward faithfulness. But those actions are not idiosyncratic and arbitrary. No matter how appropriate a ministry seems to the pastor, no matter how called one feels to accomplish a particular service, no matter how necessary such a ministry may be to the community, unless it "fits" with the parish, it will amount to nothing over time.

While a pastor at Harbor Church, I watched hundreds of thousands of tourists each summer disembark from the ferryboats and flood our little island. What a ministry awaits us here, I thought. Our church, so centrally located in the harbor area, could become a bearer of God's light to countless people. Truly God was bringing our mission field to us. In order to minister I devised a coffee house program and a summer concert series. I recruited some helpers (usually some lonely Christian college kids), decorated the place, lined up the musicians (I fed, housed, and transported them as well), arranged the publicity, and generally made it work. And it did work for a while, but as soon as I stopped putting inordinate amounts of my own personal energy into it, these programs came grinding to a halt. I was discouraged. Why had so few of my parishioners caught on to the vision? Had they no concept of mission, of faithfulness, of outreach? Were they such poor Christians as that?

While I pondered the failure of these programs, very quietly, some other ministries came into being. Out of a lay-led Bible study came the idea of holding a monthly luncheon for our elderly neighbors. Eight years later this Second Wind Luncheon was still going strong. It had no budget, no church-appointed leader, no official staff, no rules for who should attend. Somehow food and people appeared and it happened every month. Likewise, Project Harvest Share was born when a parishioner realized that his excess tomatoes and zucchinis could fill the stomachs of his shut-in neighbors. From late summer through fall, vegetables and canned goods appeared at church every Sunday and were quietly distributed to the needy on Monday. Ministry and service? Absolutely! The ones I envisioned, planned, and promoted? Absolutely not. The ones that grew out of the congregation's own concerns, they were the ones that "fit."

The small-church congregation is concerned. It does want to do mission. It does believe in outreach. But it has a particular way of understanding and acting in this area. It is not motivated by the extent of human need. It is motivated by the proximity of human need. It doesn't know how to give to a faceless person somewhere else, worthy as he or she may be. But it will bend over backward to help its own. It feels uncomfortable adopting new behaviors. (New ministries are like a foreign language, not only different but threatening and debilitating.) Yet doing what it already knows how to do for those whom it can reach is as natural as apple pie. Neighborhood surveys, census data, and other objective indices of ministry potential are irrelevant to the small church. But it would be erroneous to conclude that the small church doesn't care about outreach. Caring is not motivated or revealed the way a bureaucratic approach is, yet it is truly there. The wise leader who would enhance the doing of mission has but to assist his or her small church in putting its feelings into action. So that deed may fit compassion.

For example, consider the response when a valued member of our Harbor Church congregation had become like an irresponsible child in his aging. It hurt us to see him that way and it hurt us more to know the anguish and effort his wife underwent in caring for him. No one knew what to do. Calls offering help were politely rejected. Many parishioners asked me what could be done. I did not know. Finally a parishioner made a list of people who would visit for the afternoon or take the aging man for a ride, freeing his wife to rest, go shopping, or just be by herself. Everyone was willing to sign up, with such enthusiasm as to make a blessing out of assigning afternoons. The routine was greatly appreciated, and for weeks it went on, ministry and appreciation, service and blessing. It fit. The effort transformed the concern we all felt into a viable plan of action. After all, visiting and driving are what we'd do anyhow. This way we could do it for love. All that was needed was a form to actualize our caring.

So if you, small-church leader, would like to enhance the caring behavior of your church, do not look for mission programs or data, facts or figures. Look until you find the concern that is already in your people's hearts. And then find a familiar, comfortable way to release it, embodying it in service. Make the service fit the concern.

CONCLUSION

In this section of the book I have attempted to paint a picture of what the world looks like to people in the small church. In doing so I have made the assumption that they exhibit a folk mentality and that their social dynamics resemble those of the folk society, as described by Robert Redfield. Much of my description is hypothetical, inferential, and anecdotal. Nevertheless, I feel that it is substantially accurate. Probably no small church, or small-church person, sees the world exactly as I have described. For that matter, many large congregations and large-church folk may look at the world with some of these elements. Still, I believe that the following parameters of folk mentality, which differ markedly from those of our dominant cultural mentality, can be used to better understand what makes an actual small church tick.

The parameters of this folk mentality include the following:

- Life experience is understood as a totality.
- The social world, the flow and rhythms of time, and the aspects of behavior all cohere in an integrated pattern.
- This pattern provides a solution to the recurrent issues of life; gives a sense of well-being, of all being right in the world; and motivates individuals to maintain it.
- Behavior is motivated more from habit than intention, and changes, though difficult to achieve, can be long lived.
- Reflection is not an ordinary behavior. If an explanation is obtainable, it is usually in the form of myth, the story of a particular individual's deeds in the past. Problems are solved but more on the basis of intuition than analysis.
- Solutions tend to resemble the past, be recognized by an inner light going on, and fit the social experience of the people involved.
- The world is above all a peopled world. Reality is perceived personally and relationally.
- Time is marked by events; it is cyclical and yet is aimed toward the past.
- Space is not quantitative but is valued for social function and as a point of connection with those who have occupied it.
- The world is seen as essentially fixed and behavior is aimed at maintaining the social world.

If these characteristics are substantially accurate, as I obviously believe they are, the conclusions for leadership seem bleak indeed. That is, if leadership is seen as greater than management. I use "management" here to mean the exercising of routine decisions that are already within the thought and behavioral patterns of the social entity. "Leadership," on the other hand, means the introduction of movement in the patterns of the group in a direction that "fits" with its environment and its integrity. Thus leadership involves change. (The decision to plant corn due to depletion of prey for a nomadic, hunting tribe is "leadership.") But how can one lead in a social entity that is structured to resist change? How can one lead in such an entity when the tools of leadership are designed for organizations that view change positively? Are some leadership tools and approaches appropriate to the small-church world? These questions will be addressed in the next section.

PART THREE

Leadership in the Small Church

CHAPTER SEVEN

The Feel of Leadership: Effective Understandings and Attitudes

Do not be conformed to this world but be transformed by the renewal of your mind, that you may prove what is the will of God, what is good and acceptable and perfect. (Romans 12:2)

One of the hardest transitions for ambitious and well-trained small-church leaders is the mental one. It is difficult to view the small-church world as legitimate, as having a different integrity, a validity of its own, once one has been "conformed" to rational, future-oriented, programmatic, and quantitative thinking. But all who would understand and lead effectively in folk societies must be transformed. Anthropologist Elman Service describes this transition in his field study:

> "That's-the-way-we-do." Hearing this again was too much. I rose painfully from the squat that I assumed in imitation of my Havasupai friend when he was giving me instruction. I stomped around on my prickling legs and said in near exasperation, "But why?"
> Paya looked up at me, silent, and I saw that I was discourteous to the old man by towering over him. I squatted and waited. Everything always took so long! He watched my face as though to be sure of my full attention. I looked into his eyes—watching, waiting.
> The silence lingered, except for the sound of the falls and rapids as Havasu Creek rushed through its red-walled gorge toward the Grand Canyon. As usual, we had walked along the stream to be alone for our daily interview, away from his family and neighbors.

Finally, never blinking, his seamed face calm, Paya repeated, "That's-the-way-we-do." He spoke even more slowly than usual. His normal English was halting, with dreamy spaces often conveying as much significance as his words. This illiterate old man prized exactly expressed thought, and he did not care how long it took to achieve it: the attitude of a respected wise-man. But this phrase, spoken so softly, held me in the same way that his unwavering gaze had stilled my movements.

My introduction to Havasupai culture was also an introduction to the mind of this man, and at first I was never sure which was which. Later I realized that his careful intensity of manner stemmed from concern that I, a messenger to the outside, should understand the ways of the Havasupai—not just his own. "The way *we* do."

I discovered still later that he was trying to teach me a simple idea of great significance, which I have tried to teach others for the past twenty-five years.

In our sessions he would describe in annoying detail how to do a curing ceremony, or plant corn, recite an origin myth, or calculate kinship. I dutifully took down the information, but impatiently. This was my first fieldwork; I wanted some short cuts, generalizations; above all, I wanted to know the reasons *why* the Indians acted in their peculiar ways. Paya answered: "That's-the-way . . ." Then he would go back to the description as if I had misunderstood the whole thing.

I was looking for a key to Havasupai culture, afraid of not finding it, and right there I impatiently overlooked the truth: *There is no key to understanding another culture except on its own terms.*[1]

The small church, too, must be understood on its own terms, not on our society's or our denomination's or the business world's. It is precisely this transition that is a prerequisite for effective small-church leadership. In this section I will attempt to paint in broad strokes some of the insights and understandings (eventually leading to certain kinds of action, as we will see in the next chapters) necessary to a valid ministry in the small-church world.

READINESS OR RESISTANCE?

A new small-church pastor should not expect to make significant change immediately and easily, especially by virtue of simply being "the pastor." Most of us have been raised to think that we can make a difference. We are educated to think in terms of possibilities. We live within a society in rapid flux. Change is rapid, pervasive, accelerating. One isn't "with it" unless one is either creating change or managing it.

The college I attended boasted that it pumped out one thousand "leaders" every year. Now, leaders are those who make a difference, who affect their environment in some significant way. Leaders change things. So I sallied forth not only ready to change the world but thinking that the world was ready to be changed. I was soon to be enlightened on both points! The first few years at Harbor Church I was able to add a number of complementary programs and restore some previous activities. Yes, I was able to change certain things, but I was not able to make some fundamental changes in the congregation's priorities and ways of doing things. Sometimes it seemed that the only change I had effected was an increase in the congregation's ability to resist change! How much anguish I could have been spared had I expected resistance instead of readiness.

The small-church world does not change easily. Nurturing progress in a small church is a difficult job. It takes time. It takes love. It takes blood, sweat, and tears. If you aspire to move a small-church congregation, be prepared to perspire.

At Harbor Church I had a one-sentence goal for both my parish's mission commitment and my pastoral ministry efforts: to participate with God in the transformation of human life from its present state toward the individual, corporate, and institutional fullness of our divine destiny. "Individual, corporate, and institutional" reminded me to keep broad and balanced in my concern for faithfulness and righteousness. "To participate with God" kept me humble. It reminded me that only as God is at work will true progress be made. I can be a channel but not a source of eternity becoming real here and now.

"The transformation of human life" kept me on track. The goal of ministry is not production. It is not running programs, raising funds, and erecting buildings. The goal of ministry is the transformation of human beings (including myself!). Production can be defined and monitored. Transformation can only be glimpsed and nurtured. Production can be scheduled.

Transformation is born in eternity and enters our experience in ways we can't predict or control. Production can be accomplished quickly. Transformation takes a long time.

The desire to accomplish a lot quickly results in no lasting effect. There is a pond near our house which our family uses for boating and bathing. When boating I repeatedly push against the waters of the pond with the oars. This, I have noticed, has very little effect on the pond—a few short-lived ripples, but not even a hole where the oar once was. Of course, this pushing moves the boat (while keeping it above water), but the pond remains unchanged.

We also bathe in the pond. We splash around, swim out over our heads, and feel its buoyancy, warmth, and refreshment. We have made some changes in the pond: cleared away some weeds, raked the rocks away from a ten-foot beach, made it more inviting. But it took a while and we had to get our feet wet to do it. It is the same in the small church. One can pastor energetically, rapidly, and from above, making a few waves that have no lasting effect except to move oneself along. Or one can lead from within by loving, by giving oneself to the "pond."

I know a pastor who moved his congregation out of the back pews and down to the front of the sanctuary where he preached from a small lectern. He accomplished this move in one week. "One week, really?" I asked him. "Yep, one week. 'Course it took me twelve years to build up the trust and the sense of mutuality to allow it to happen!"

God doesn't seem to be in a hurry. If after 2,000 years God is still working on transforming humankind, what do we really think we can accomplish in a week, a month, or a year? Maybe we should think more in terms of generations.

The small church is an inertial organization, not an intentional one. It goes merrily along in the direction in which it is heading, not necessarily in the direction we think it ought to be going. This built-in inertia makes it difficult to change directions. But it is also the reason it has survived so long against difficult odds. It does not live on the level of rationality and decision making. It lives on the level of habit and the heart.

Effective leadership in the small church can be very difficult, can take time, and can best be accomplished from within. Wise small-church leaders realize that to be effective we must be in it for the long haul.

IN OR OUT?

Wise small-church leaders must be able to live in and enjoy the small-church world without being trapped in it. We must be part of the people for our leadership to be accepted and appropriate, but not so much a part of the small-church world that we offer no impetus to greater faithfulness.

The doctorate of ministry program in which I was enrolled required me to define a ministry "issue" at my church, then the Harbor Church on Block Island. After writing up the nature of the problem, its history, causes, and so on, I started to share it with a committee from the congregation. We weren't five minutes into this session when I noticed Barbara was frowning. Barbara was chairing the deacons that year. She had been a trustee for more than a decade and had organized almost every social function at the church. What Barbara didn't know about the church wasn't worth knowing. So when Barbara frowned, I frowned. Then her frown deepened. The more she read, the more she frowned. She looked discouraged and then visibly upset. I started to worry. Had I been way off base in my assessment of the needs in the church? Had I been too heavy handed in my description of the problem? "Barbara, what's the matter?" I asked. "Am I wrong in the way I have sized things up?" She paused and sighed. "No, no. It's all true. I just hate to see it in black and white."

For Barbara our church was like family. We had problems, certainly, and we were aware of them. We knew them in our hearts and in our guts. We lived with them and we changed what we could. But we didn't think of them in a detached, clinical, objective way, as if we could have divorced the problem. And we certainly didn't tell the neighbors about it. That would have been going too far.

In writing up our church's problems for the seminary, I had gone over the line. In expressing objectively what we all knew subjectively, I had placed myself outside the identity of the group. I had put myself against them. This was not a welcome activity. It threatened the group, and Barbara was sensitive and honest enough to say so. My movement from a pastor inside the small church to a critic outside the group exposed a vulnerability: it laid bare the members' frailties and foibles. Had I persisted, it would have led to "irrational" behavior on their part to defend themselves from me.

Defensiveness is an ancient and fundamental response ("I was afraid because I was naked; so I hid," Gen. 3:10). It can occur when criticism is neither communicated nor even intended. When changes, such as new mission programs, are suggested by one not central to the group, the response is not to weigh the proposal objectively against the needs and resources of the group. The response is "What's the matter, we're not good enough for you as we are?" or "Take us as you find us," or "Pay your dues before you nominate yourself president." Maybe there is no verbal response at all (or perhaps even a mild positive one), but in 1,001 ways the new program is resisted and/or sabotaged. Thus we are associated with failure ("We told you it wouldn't work. We tried that once before," or "See, we were right all along"). It is seldom productive to threaten the identity of the group.

Nevertheless, faithful small-church leaders must not equate the kingdom of God with the present state of the congregation. One cannot live completely within the little world of the small church and be true to one's calling as pastor. We must be able to "step out" once in a while, to look biblically and objectively at our tribe, to set our sights on God's intentions for the congregation. But then we need to step back inside the small-church world. Certain prophets of Israel were able to measure the tribes against the scale of eternity. When they stepped out they found Israel wanting, but they didn't step back in. They literally became a voice crying in the wilderness. Their pleas are as appropriate today as they were originally, possibly because they had so little success in getting anybody to see things their way.

Faithful small-church leaders must neither march self-righteously into the role of external critic—little true ministry occurs from that position— nor slip into the small-church world so totally as to lose sight of eternity. We must live with a tension most of our people will not have to live with. We must live inside and outside of the small-church world, with one foot in each.

BACKWARD OR FORWARD?

One of the small prop planes that flies to Block Island is a six-seater with the two middle seats facing backward. This creates a cozy foursome for conversation during the fifteen-minute flight from the mainland. Nevertheless, I avoid these rear-facing seats if at all possible. I find it disorienting and uncomfortable to not be facing where I am going. I don't like to be looking at where I've been. I want to be keyed in on where I'm heading. I like to have my sights set on my goals. The forward look. This is what progress and leadership are all about.

There are two problems with the forward look for small-church leaders, however. First, it is not how life is actually lived. Second, small-church people find it an uncomfortable way to live life. For some reason known only to the divinity, God created time (as opposed to space) to be unidirectional. We can know the happenings of the past, but we cannot know the future. We do move forward in time, but we don't really know where we are going. We can plan, prepare, predict, pro-act, but we can never know where we will be until we've gotten there. Intentionality, goal setting, and strategizing are means of making desirable potential outcomes more probable. But we know only where we have been. We can only be certain of the past. The backward look is the only perspective that sees reality. The forward look is an illusion based on intention. It may create a reality, but it is not a reality. We can move forward in time only on the basis of the past, on the basis of history and experience.

So the backward look sees reality, a reality with which small-church people are comfortable. The past is home. Tradition is the method of operating. "The way we have done things before" is the way we want to do them. Small-church people know these ways, feel comfortable with these ways, see these as the "right" ways, and know ourselves as the enactors of these ways.

In the abstract of Redfield's "The Folk Society" he describes the content of the article:

> Such a society is small, isolated, nonliterate, and homogeneous, with a strong sense of group solidarity. The ways of living are conventionalized into that coherent system which we call "a culture." Behavior is traditional, spontaneous, uncritical, and personal; there is no legislation or habit of experiment and reflection for intellectual ends. Kinship, its relationships and institutions, are the type categories of experience and the familial group is the unit of action. The sacred prevails over the secular; the economy is one of status rather than of the market. These and related characterizations may be restated in terms of "folk mentality."[2]

So the folk society is seen in a small grouping of people who know each other well. They have a past that includes each other. Their history is a shared history. Thus one aspect of their past is its personal nature. The past that is functional in the folk society is limited because the true folk society is illiterate and has little contact with other peoples. The past is what is remembered in the minds and the oral traditions of its members. So the past becomes present reality in the folk-society culture.

> The ways in which the members of the society meet the recurrent problems of life are conventionalized ways; they are the results of long intercommunication within the group in the face of these problems and these conventionalized ways have become interrelated within one another so that they constitute a coherent and self-consistent system. Such a system is what we mean in saying that the folk society is characterized by "a culture." A culture is an organization or integration of conventional understandings. It is, as well, the acts and the objects, in so far as they represent the type characteristic of that society, which express and maintain these understandings. In the folk society this integrated whole, this system, provides for all the recurrent needs of the individual from birth to death and of the society through the seasons and the years.[3]

The way in which things are done in a folk society is another way in which the past is determinative of the present.

> What is done in the ideal folk society is done not because somebody or some people decided, at once, that it should be done, but because it seems "necessarily" to flow from the very nature of things. There is, moreover, no disposition to reflect upon traditional acts and consider them objectively and critically. In short, behavior in the folk society is traditional, spontaneous, and uncritical.[4]

The way in which the past has determined the present goes a long way toward shaping the future. "The interrelations and high degree of consistency among the elements of custom which are presented to the individual declare to him the importance of making his endeavors in the direction indicated by tradition."[5] In addition, the ways of the past are not only comfortable, but they came to be endowed with a moral rectitude above and beyond their functionality.

The ways of life are folkways; furthermore, the folkways tend to be also mores—ways of doing or thinking to which attach notions of moral worth. The value of every traditional act or object or institution is, thus, something which the members of the society are not disposed to call into question; and should the value be called into question the doing so is resented. This characteristic of the folk society may be briefly referred to by saying that it is a sacred society. In the folk society one may not, without calling into effect negative social sanctions, challenge as valueless what has come to be traditional in that society.[6]

We have in Redfield's description a society which operates in a very short time frame, whose past is preserved by means of oral traditions, habituated behavior, and conventionalized thought patterns brought into the present in such a way as to almost make a unity of the two, and whose future looks very much like a mirror image of its past. In such a society the past becomes the present and predicts the future by means of some combination of folk traditions and oral history, myth sharing, story telling, habitual behavior, and a conventionalized worldview. It is particularly important to note the degree to which moral rightness and sacredness inhere in the past made present. In other words, the past, our traditions, are not only the way we are today but also the way we must be. With the exception of an utterly debilitating crisis situation, it appears as though change and renewal are hardly possible in such a society.

What about renewal and the past in this type of society? We may conclude that change is very difficult to achieve in such a social entity. It will be resisted as not only alien but also as immoral, as indeed it is from an internal perspective. But to the degree that renewal, adaptation, and change are possible, they cannot be conceived as occurring through a rational attempt to apprehend the future. Rather, they must come as aspects of the past. The change must sound like what we believed all along and it must look like who we have been all along.

However comfortable and appropriate the backward look may be for small-church people, it is not an adequate perspective for leadership. Only in the case of a social grouping perfectly adapted to a static environment would looking backward be an adequate leadership style. I doubt that such a case has ever existed. It certainly does not for today's small-church leader. Effective leadership in the small church today must be able to look forward.

Such leaders must be able to perceive social and demographic trends. Such leaders must register changes within the congregation itself. Such leaders must be alert to new needs and hurts in their communities. Such leaders must hear anew the voice of Christ calling in the "least of these my brethren."

But such leaders must not expect to persuade small-church people to respond on the basis of a forward look. Rather, such leaders can expect the forward look to be disorienting and debilitating. To the degree that it is registered, it feels like a lament, not a call. "Things aren't the way they used to be [in the 'good old days']." "I hardly know anybody here any more." (This comment was overheard after a pastor welcomed six new people into membership in a small church!)

The forward look is the function of leadership, not a function of the whole body of the small church. Having looked forward, effective small-church leaders have just begun. We must now step back into the world of history and heritage, memory and tradition. We must scan the past for values and behaviors that are appropriate for the future. These we must cultivate and nurture. By utilizing the backward look of the congregation, we lead forward.

This is a significantly different enterprise than planning in a rational organization. It embodies different values. It utilizes different strategies. Effective small-church leaders must be willing to live with a sprained neck, but we must not think we can lead by looking forward only.

REFLEXIVE OR REFLECTIVE?

To effectively lead a small church we need to disabuse ourselves of two notions of leadership. The first is that a small-church pastor sits atop the congregation the way a general sits atop his troops. The small church is not a pyramid of power with the pastor at the apex. "Orders" barked by small-church pastors are much more likely to be disobeyed or ignored than to be obeyed. "Lording over" Christ's followers is not a faithful leadership posture.

Neither is the opposite assumption, that is, that without leadership activity the body of believers themselves will respond adequately to ensure their internal health and external mission. The small church, as we have argued, is an inertial organization. It will keep going in a preset direction, virtually in isolation from the movement of the environment. Unless adjustments are made, over time acting from either of these two notions will result in a mismatch between the church and its context.

The repertoire of behaviors available to a small church decreases over time unless new behaviors are introduced. This I learned at Harbor Church when I selected a new hymn to be sung at worship. The complaints after the service were louder than the singing of the hymn! Precious little effort was made to acquaint me with the congregation's favorites, nor did I attempt to compile such a list on my own. Instead I picked hymns with which I was familiar, thinking they'd also be familiar to the congregation. This led to the worst of both worlds: a negative reaction from the parish and the absence of the joy and comfort ordinarily engendered by familiar lyrics and tunes. Consequently we ended up singing from a very narrow band of hymns, a great loss for all of us. Eventually, realizing this dynamic, I moved to overcome it. But that is the point: the natural dynamics of an inertial organization lead to diminution. Leadership activity is necessary to stay open to God's riches.

How are we to understand the nature of this activity and its dynamics? Consider a simple model drawn from biology. (Note: This and the following models are meant to be evocative of differing leadership approaches. They are not meant to be pushed regarding detail.)

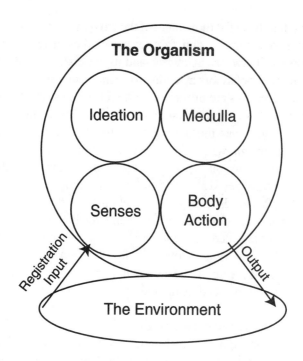

The environment is the world beyond the organism. For the small church the environment may be the community or neighborhood, the denomination, and particular sets of relationships that have developed over time. Inputs (changes, resources, and so on) are registered by the small church in its sensory function. The brain is the locus of ideational response, typically, rational, logical, future oriented, and programmatic. For our purposes the medulla may be considered the locus of "instinct." It is the place where spontaneous, uncritical, unreflective impetus for action originates. The body is the arms, hands, legs, lips, ears, and so on, which actually minister to the world. This is the agency of output into the environment, the "doers of the word."

The two dysfunctional leadership postures in the small church are "the general" and "instinct." Instinct is functional in a static environment, not what exists in today's world. The leadership posture I have dubbed "the general" is one that is very appealing and seductive to many pastors. Wouldn't we all like to simply issue orders and have our laity jump to carry them out! The result, however, is not obedience or even compliance; it is alienation, withdrawal, conflict, or clergy termination. Small congregations, especially, want to be loved, not bossed around. They want to be respected far more than they want to be directed. They have a functional integrity that is minimized by the general. And the general's assumption that he or she knows best is often patently untrue! In some ways "instinct" leadership is the polar opposite of leadership by "the general." Instinct is based simply on doing things as they have always been done without any adjustment caused by environmental changes. The diagrams of these two postures:

"The General"

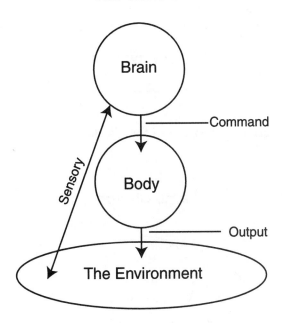

"Instinct"

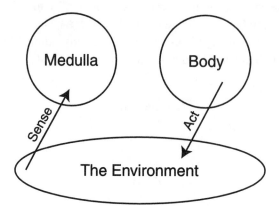

What I presume to be a model for a healthy large church is:

"Large Church"

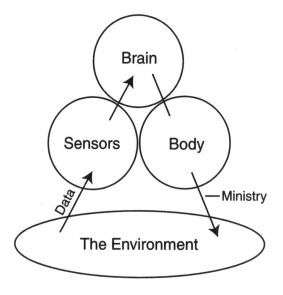

What I would propose for the small church looks like this:

"Small Church"

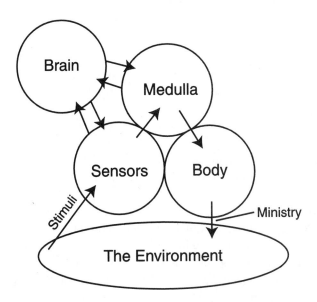

As an organism the small church is more reflexive than reflective. It senses needs in the environment and responds in ways that have proved effective and meaningful in the past. In the vast majority of cases this is both helpful and efficient. Reflexive ministry does a lot of good quickly and comfortably because both giver and receiver have come to expect that type of help. At Harbor Church, for example, it was not uncommon for me to go to the hospital on the mainland to visit a sick parishioner or islander and find the hospital room wall literally covered with get-well cards. "It is so, so encouraging," one parishioner said with tears in his eyes, "to know so many people are thinking of me and praying for me. It does my heart good." Our congregational card mailing was a reflexive ministry: we didn't invent it each time, it was just part of who we were and how we expressed our love. And we had many more: after-funeral luncheons, Christmas caroling, shut-in visitations, seniors' luncheons, and so on. Christ's love was made real in every one of these ministries.

But not all ministry is as it has been since the time of our forefathers. It has been speculated that more change occurred in the twentieth century than in all the previous centuries combined. The situation is still changing. New needs and ministry opportunities are arising. The faithful small church will be called to minister to a changing community. But how can it do something incongruent with its reflexive nature?

Effective small-church leaders know that we are working with a reflexive organization. We also know that we are not dealing with a reflective one. It is not that small-church people do not or cannot think. Some of the world's wisest people are small-church people. Rather, it is that small-church people do not consider thinking—rational, abstracted, and impersonal—a particularly helpful tool for the solution of life's ongoing issues. In addition, small-church people may have a weaker comprehension of the existence of "new" needs (that is, those for which reflexive solutions are not adequate) or may be fearful, an intuitive sense of impotency, in the face of "new" problems.

Here is where effective small-church leaders can function for greater faithfulness. We can dream about new behaviors that will result in greater health, faithfulness, and ministry in the congregation. But—and this is most important—if those dreams are to become reality and are to be sustained as a ministry, they must become reflexes. The small church is not interested in reinventing its ministries at each annual business meeting. It understands faithfulness not as being innovative but as being constant. So new and appropriate ministry programs need to become part of our identity, part of who we are. This function of leadership—the creation of new responses, behaviors, reflexes—is a sporadic, indirect, hidden activity.

It is sporadic, not regular. It is like salt, delicious as a seasoning but ghastly as a main course! It should be engaged in as needed: to respond to a new situation, to correct an oversight or weakness, and so on. But to think that the small church can be rationally redesigned periodically is to misunderstand its nature completely.

It is indirect in that, for maximum effectiveness over time, it must become a reflex, not simply an activity. This requires a shift in focus from the product (ministry) to the producer (ministers). Pushing to achieve an outcome is a one-time enterprise. Building a new reflex within the life of the people is slower and less straightforward, but it is more satisfying. It can sometimes be accomplished by cloning, eliciting a behavior similar to an existing behavior, or by kaleidoscoping, rearranging a set of familiar behaviors into a new pattern. (More on this in the following chapters.)

It is a hidden activity. It cannot be done with trumpets and fireworks. The more its development is quiet, simple, and behind the scenes, the more likely its success. And the more limited the role of the initiator, the more likely its long-term viability. Leaders who sense a need, create a solution, and implement the ministry alone are more likely to be burned out than to be of benefit. The response that is widely felt and broadly enacted out of generalized concern, on the other hand, is well on its way to becoming a reflex.

Programs can be credited to creators; reflexes must be everyone's child. I learned this the hard way. I once proposed a Sunday School addition on the south wall of Fellowship Hall at Harbor Church. It was soundly and noisily rejected at our annual meeting. I got more "guff" for that proposal than for any ten of my other best "worst ideas." "Tony's addition" became synonymous with "ridiculousness." Time went by until eventually the proposal was forgotten. But the issue remained: where to put our growing Sunday School? The trustees considered various options. The addition was put on the list. Less feasible alternatives withered. The addition remained. Finally it was deemed the best. It was duly explained by the trustees and approved overwhelmingly at our annual meeting four years after it was derisively rejected. In those four years it had been forgotten that I proposed it. It had been forgotten how unfeasible it once seemed. It had gone from a foolish, impossible idea to one of many ideas, to a good idea, to the best idea. No one remembered that it was my idea. In fact, someone mentioned that a trustee subcommittee came up with the idea twenty-five years ago! That was fine, since the Sunday School got the space it needed.

Spear Waving or Sticking to the Subject?

In *Return to Laughter* Bowen recounts her experiences among the tribesmen of the African bush. Her description of how conflict is resolved and how decisions are made is fascinating and insightful.

> There was a long wait, while more and more elders came. I located Ikpoom. He told me that a woman married into this homestead had died in the night; she had five children; the strangers were her relatives; she would be buried today. . . . I was prepared for ritual, for funeral orations perhaps, for anything but what actually happened. It was a debate, conducted with all the noise and

irreverence of a court case. And I understood not one word of it.
First the strangers orated. Kako and his elders objected to everything they said. The strangers spoke even more hotly. En masse,
they advanced to the center of the yard. The notables . . . marched
grimly out into the yard. Old men stuck out their chins pugna-
ciously; they shouted and waved their barbed spears in menacing
gesticulation. . . . Finally Kako and some of his elders, either convinced or outshouted, returned to our tree and sat down again. Not
Yabo. He, Poorgbilin and a few others were still arguing and bran-
dishing their spears in dangerous persuasion. It looked like the
beginning of a fight; I hoped it was merely their style of rhetoric.
Kako tried to quiet Yabo, who turned upon him with a snarl. Kako
jumped up, backed by his followers. He and Yabo argued bitterly.
Meanwhile, the strangers unobtrusively and prudently withdrew
to their own tree.[7]

And, on a second occasion:

Yabo and Poorgbilin had the same great grandfather. The day's
business could not be settled unless all the male descendents of
that ancestor were present. They could continue to ostracize Yabo
only by slighting their own and pressing business. People here
lived so closely together that almost every movement of one irri-
tated another. Yet they were so dependent on each other that
continuing a feud or indulging a spite was a luxury taxed with
personal disadvantage. Yabo was called to the meeting and came.
At first, he was treated to . . . cold civility. . . .

However, the polite manner is incompatible with their debating
technique. One cannot shout and brandish a spear with reserve.
Inevitably, as soon as people began to find their interests threatened, they began to stamp and scream. Yabo was out in the middle,
yelling with the best of them. It was an angry scene, but a very
normal one. Yabo, I felt, was back in.[8]

I have a theological degree from two separate seminaries. For each
degree I took courses in church administration, dealing with how to handle
governing committees or deacon boards. Forming agendas, setting priorities, directing discussions, gaining consensus, minimizing diversions, assigning tasks, delegating responsibilities, eliminating tangents—these were some

of the wonderful things I learned how to do. And I found that these things worked reasonably well on a national task force I chaired. The members of the task force met every six months, had little interaction between meetings, weren't exactly sure why we were meeting, and didn't know what to expect from our meetings, but were highly motivated once the meeting was called to order. The task force members were, by and large, willing to stick to the subject once it was specified. Of course, it took three years to figure out the specification!

Members of the Harbor Church governing boards were not confused about why they were meeting. They might not have been able to put it into words, but they knew in their hearts. They did not need my administration to stick to the subject. Their life together was the subject. And they stuck to it in their own way. But when people live in close proximity week in and week out for decades, with the prospect of decades more, the ways of doing things are different. The task agenda is the lesser agenda. The relationship agenda is the greater concern.

Small-church people have to live together. We have to live with ourselves and with each other. This leads to seemingly contradictory behaviors. In order to live with each other we sometimes have to go sit under a tree and be quiet, to use Bowen's image. In order to live with ourselves we sometimes have to yell and scream, stomp and jump, and wave our spears.

Spear waving may be "an angry scene," but it is also "a very normal one." Spear waving has its healthy aspects. It ensures that every position is heard and every ego is accounted for. It clears the air and gives each member a say. And it clearly reveals who is invested in the issue, in the church, in the common life. It allows people to move from the emotional agenda to the objective one, from the relational to content.

Effective small-church leaders do not fear spear waving. (Two extremes may be cause for concern, however: No spear waving indicates no investment. And excessive spear waving, indicating too much investment, can lead to interpersonal violence and need not be tolerated.) Rather, we see it as a means of allowing people to live together over time. Once spear waving serves its function, leadership can be exerted. Each side can be shown how at least some of their concerns are embodied in a course of action to be taken. Each side can feel that its position was at least heard. Each side may be "spent" enough after the spear waving to heed the leader's temperate approach. It takes leadership abilities beyond "agenda-izing." It takes real creativity and sensitivity. It is challenging, to be sure, but it is also fun.

Another story from Harbor Church—the "hanging" of Nathan Mott—illustrates this dynamic. Nathan Mott was an island sea captain who invested his fortune in a hotel in 1885. Through various bequests that hotel had become the present church building. Some of the members remembered Nathan Mott and thought it appropriate that his portrait hang in the church's vestibule. After all, if it were not for Nathan, we would not have had a church (building). Others wondered for years who that old man hanging in the vestibule was. When the vestibule was repainted Nathan was put away for "safe keeping." After a couple of years his absence was noticed by three older parishioners. These women were seen meeting together to discuss this problem. After a while the trustee chair was taken to task for displacing this portrait, but he could not see why the picture of Jesus that now hung there was of less importance to the church than Nathan. Finally, after a few more discussions, he agreed to rehang Nathan. He did so, but in a new spot behind the door opening up to the balcony. That would never do for the three parishioners. It would have to do, according to our trustee. Level by level the tension mounted, our parishioners making their demands ever more loudly, our trustee denying them ever more adamantly. Enter the pastor with a proposal to create a display regarding our whole heritage of faith with the portrait of Nathan one part thereof. Motion approved. Nathan was rehung pending the complete display. Now we could sit under our trees until the next time we needed to wave our spears.

SEEING OR BELIEVING?

"Seeing is believing," the expression goes. Thomas wouldn't believe that Jesus had been raised from the dead until he saw the imprint of the nails on Jesus' hands and feet. But believing leads to seeing just as much as the reverse. Believing in a new reality, envisioning a different future, dreaming of a new tomorrow, is often the first step in its realization. Believing is seeing, too.

"I'm not going to believe it until I see it for myself," most people in the small church would say. To the apostle John small-church people would say, "We know that which 'we have heard, which we have seen with our eyes, which we have looked upon and touched with our hands'" (1 John 1:1). Like Thomas, we aren't going to believe anything new until we see it. Things are as they have been. New things are not believed until they have been experienced. Most small-church people give credence to the body's eye, not the mind's eye. Precious few of us can envision new realities; fewer still can hear the Lord calling us forth into a land that we have never seen.

This reality poses a challenge for small-church leaders when changes, perceived as more than refinements, are at stake. How can movement be encouraged in this situation? A revealing incident occurred with the Harbor Church Renovations Committee. I had tried to constitute this committee as broadly and as representatively as possible. Every facet of the life of the church was reflected in this group, which was to oversee the remodeling of our Fellowship Hall, kitchen, and Sunday School areas. I figured that whatever we could hammer out would enjoy relatively smooth sailing with the rest of the congregation, but I hadn't figured on how hard it would be to hammer things out in this committee. From the beginning of our discussion on remodeling the kitchen, peculiar behavior occurred. Even though an existing floor plan with two possible remodelings, all drawn to scale, were on blueprints in front of us, people would leave the meeting, walk next door to the kitchen area, and return in a couple of minutes. One by one they went until they had all gone at least once. Then two by two, then groups at a time. The meeting began to resemble musical chairs! Finally, I got up and joined the parade to find that each one was pacing around the kitchen trying to "see" what the proposed changes would really be like! It was obvious that the blueprints did little to help them envision the new kitchen; they had to go to the spot and "feel" it.

If that got us off to a flying start, the second meeting went downhill from there. Tension filled the air from the opening prayer. Every proposed improvement in the kitchen was objected to, deemed irrelevant, or otherwise resisted. What confounded me was that the one who was objecting the most was the one I thought would most benefit from the changes. It was the woman who, with great personal effort, organized the crews to work in the kitchen for our big fund-raising dinners. "I don't see why we need more space," she said. "We get along fine as it is." (Workers during big dinners were so tightly packed into our home-sized kitchen that to get another platter of potatoes to serve in the dining hall, a bucket brigade had to be formed, for literally not one more person could be squeezed into the kitchen!) "And you can't make that the clean-up area. That's where we serve the cranberry sauce from." Evidently the new and efficient cranberry-serving spot had gone unnoticed. In fact, the problem, the new floor plan, and even the need for the plan were just plain not seen.

Although I desperately wanted her input and blessing of the planned changes, she ceased coming to meetings. "No sense causing a fight," she said. In fact, the whole group shrunk down to an unrepresentative handful who could see where the rub was and could envision ways to change things. Finally the plans were approved and the kitchen renovated. With fear and trepidation I awaited the coming of our first big dinner in the new kitchen. Surprisingly things went without a hitch! The next day the organizer saw me downtown and started flapping her arms, with an amazing likeness to a chicken. For the life of me, I couldn't figure out what was up. "Didn't the dinner go great?" she asked. "And it was so pleasant having plenty of room to work in." (Thus the arm movements.) Apparently she took my chin dropping to the ground as agreement, and went merrily on her way. She is a wonderful Christian and a very hard worker for Christ's church. She just sees things by experiencing them, not by envisioning them!

I had come into the pastorate believing consensus to be the Christian method of operating. Failing that in important areas, the majority was to rule. How much time I wasted, how much energy I lost, how many feelings I hurt trying to persuade people beforehand of a greater good! I learned that it is only by experiencing that a judgment can be made, and it is only after personal involvement that evaluation can be accomplished.

Very few people in small-church culture can envision the significant new things that God is calling us to. Is this what the apostle Paul meant when he said that some have the gift of faith? Effective small-church leaders will not bother with the nearly futile exercise of trying to get all or the majority to agree a priori with a change, but rather will work with the one or two or three who can "see" what is yet to be. When the vision has become tangible enough for others to "see," it will be incorporated into the body or it will be rejected, just as the human body accepts or rejects an organ. For people who know, not by thinking and projecting but by experiencing, only at that point can a fair and informed decision be made. Effective leaders will allow them that input before "calling the question."

In my experience two further things occur if a change is accepted: (1) A precedent will be found. "Oh, it's nothing new. Not really. Remember when Pastor Time-Out-Of-Mind was here? We did something about that then. That's when . . ." (there follows a story). (2) Those whose only input was negative become some of the loudest evangelists of the change. The thing they opposed with boundless energy is that of which they are now as proud as peacocks! I don't understand this dynamic, but it reminds me of the hockey player who, after giving up the winning goal, praised the scorer: "He has to be a darn good player to get one past me." In the small church it must be a darn good idea to get it past the preservers of our equilibrium!

Summary

Someone once quipped that if you give a person a hammer, it is amazing what he or she will find to pound on. The tools at one's disposal, more than the needs of the situation, determine behavior. The hammer is a great tool, but sometimes a saw or shovel or telescope or word processor is more appropriate to the enterprise. Through our educational activities, our culture, and the potency of the corporate approach in our society, most of us have been given tools that work in a rationally organized, bureaucratically structured, forward-looking organization. To minister effectively in the small church, however, another set of tools is necessary. The attitude and approach of small-church leaders are the most basic of our leadership tools. To the degree that we are in accord with the nature of the small church's social structuring, we will be effective. In summary, following are six qualities of the small church and six corresponding attitudes:

1. *The small church is a stable, not a dynamic, organization.* Its nature is to replicate, not rethink, its previous patterns of behavior. Therefore effective small-church leaders will be aware that change is difficult to achieve and that it will take a longer time than it would in a rationally structured organization. Effective small-church leaders will realize that we are in it for the long haul. We should not be discouraged by the pace but rather should be encouraged by the fact that a new good, once in place, may live "forever."

2. *The typical small church is in a "little world unto itself."* This world is satisfying and meaningful to those within. But it is not self-correcting, nor is it even aware of itself objectively. It is difficult to change from the outside, and it is difficult to determine from the inside the path of greater faithfulness to Christ. Since both of these functions are necessary for effective leadership, such leaders must learn to live with the tension of living both inside and outside the world of the congregation.

3. *The typical small church sees the past not the future.* It registers what has been, not what can be. Because leadership involves orienting

people to the future, effective small-church leaders must be ready and willing to value the past, not only for its own merit but also as a tool for the future. Those who are unwilling to look backward in order to move forward had better have a high tolerance for frustration.

4. *The typical small church functions out of reflex and habit, not from goals and strategies rationally defined.* Therefore ministry in a small church does not so much concern getting the job done as it does building up good habits, ingrained behavioral patterns. Effective small-church leaders must be comfortable with secondary and indirect activity, transformation not production.

5. *The typical small church lives on the level of relationships, not tasks.* These relationships require work: they must be kept balanced and livable. A lot of energy is expended toward this end. Every task proposed has not only its own merits but also the possibility of upsetting relational balance. Small-church people will react to restore homeostasis. Effective small-church leaders will recognize this for what it is and accept it as a natural and necessary phenomenon, and will try to keep it within bounds and will not lose sight of the task because of it.

6. *The typical small church lives on the experiential, not the theoretical, level.* Effective small-church leaders will find ways to incorporate change into people's experience and will work with the few who can envision change. We should be less concerned with the purity of consensus or majority rule than with the practicality of giving our people a taste of what lies ahead.

Small church leaders who desire to be effective will find it helpful to cultivate these attitudes in themselves. But it is also important to have a clear-headed assessment of the health of the congregation if one is to bring these attitudes to bear where a congregation needs ministry. So let us turn our attention to congregational health.

CHAPTER EIGHT

Assessing Congregational Health

The group sat in silence, stunned. The pastor had just finished a well-articulated proposal to decrease his salary and time commitment from full time to half time. The fifteen leaders of this small church, in effect a committee representing the whole congregation, shuffled their feet and looked at their hands. Some were angry. The pastor had revealed to them their failure: their financial failure to keep their church a "full-time" church, their failure to legitimize their congregation by having a full-time pastor. Some were flat-out relieved. The financial pressure would soon be off, without having to confront the pastor; he'd done the dirty work himself! Some were concerned. The congregation might jump at this quick fix, avoiding some of the hard work presented by this financial crisis and missing the potential blessing hidden within.

Finally the silence was broken. "Well, this is a discouraging place to have come to, but there is one positive. I am convinced that one reason visitors do not often return is that they sense our anxiety about our financial condition. It doesn't feel good to them. It scares them away. Now we have the chance to create a more positive climate."

This comment was very insightful. The congregation had sacrificed corporate health by fixating on an unrealistic goal. They had allowed a disease to creep in and decrease their well-being. Ironically, their anxiety about having a full-time pastor was actually pushing them farther away from achieving that goal.

Congregational health is a difficult thing to measure. There are neither standards nor tests that give a digital readout: congregational temperature 98.6 degrees and steady, or 104 and rising. Of course, extreme ill health is palpable. Blatant conflict, complete apathy, or severe dysfunction is hard to miss. But for most congregations health is a relative reality, discerned by spiritual sensitivity informed by indicators. This chapter provides some of those indicators, with the understanding that this is art, not science. The spiritual capacity of the leader is indispensable.

"Tony," you might ask, "if congregational health is such a slippery thing, why bother with it at all?" There are reasons. The theological reason is that Jesus was spiritually healthy. As his body, congregations are called to incarnate his well-being. Churches are called by God to be sources of health for persons, families, communities, and society. If we are sick, what good are we? The psychological reason is that sick churches are hellish places to be. "They sense our anxiety." In some of the churches I work with regarding health issues, it is commonplace to hear members say, "I grit my teeth when I come to church, it is so tense around here," or "I used to enjoy church, but now it is no fun at all." We should be experiencing little bits of heaven in our congregations. The sociological reason is that health begets health and sickness begets sickness. Jesus said that he who has will get more and he who has not will lose even what he has (see Luke 8:18). This passage bothered me until I realized Jesus was simply describing the way things work. Just as healthy persons tend to grow in maturity, wisdom and spirituality, so healthy congregations build upon their health to become even stronger. Churches with significant dysfunction tend to spiral downward over time. The last reason has to do with growth and fulfilling the great commission. "They sense our anxiety . . . and it scares them away." Healthy vibes attract; sick vibes repel. I know churches where even the marginally healthy have bailed out. Guess who is left. Conversely, churches that exhibit signs of health attract others who are at that level or aspire to be.

Congregational health, I believe, is the single most critical variable in predicting a church's future. Healthy churches will serve and grow and survive and thrive and adapt, and have fun doing it. Ill congregations won't. Our regional judicatory staff is so convinced of this reality that we have focused our mission "to grow healthy churches." Churches that are growing in health have a great future. Churches that are waning in health will wane in everything else, too. Leaders, pastoral and lay, are called to be sources of health. We are called to assess areas and levels of health. We need to reinforce that which is healthy and address areas of dysfunction with the goal of redemption and rehabilitation.

Let us consider, then, five areas of congregational health: spiritual vitality, calling, common life, mission, and leadership. Obviously, the distinction between these areas is not rigid. Nor are these areas comprehensive.

But they provide enough handles to get started in the quest for greater congregational health in our small churches.

SPIRITUAL VITALITY

Much of the content of this volume examines the social dynamics of the divinely unique creation we call the "small church." I believe that the structure of the small church can embody the living presence of God in a distinct and wonderful way. But the unique capacity of the small church to be God's tribe is wasted unless the Spirit of the living God incarnates it. Thus the primary measure of congregational health is spiritual vitality. There are ten indicators that can help to identify the depth and character of the spirituality of a congregation.

1. *Language.* Is there any God/Christ talk? Too much? Many small-church members are more comfortable simply living our lives faithfully than talking about the depths of our faith. Yet if there is a deep faith within, it will find expression in some form. Our faith is good news, after all. A congregation that cannot talk about the presence and movement of God in its midst probably does not have anything to say. On the other hand, congregants who are constantly spouting theological formulas may not have any substance behind their babbling. God, ever moving forward, may have gotten away from those choosing to stay in their comfort zones, and so they are left with only a verbal vestige of the divine. Listen. God-talk is very revealing.

One of my small churches has an interesting twist on God talk. The members give wonderful, moving testimonies of God's work in their individual lives but are strangely silent about God's work in their congregation. This fact gives mute testimony to their sense of being abandoned by God after some exciting dreams failed to come to fruition twenty-five years ago. Only recently, after being able to articulate a vision for a new ministry in a new direction, have they started talking about God's presence in their midst, giving hope for the future!

2. *Changes.* What changes have occurred in the last five years? Are they perceived as enervating or as exciting? A healthy congregation not only lets new ways in but also incorporates many into its patterns of life. Are there new members on the church's governing board? How many new

hymns or choruses have been learned? Has the time of worship ever changed? Has the order of service evolved lately? Have any new ministry efforts been born recently? And so on.

3. *Patterns*. Does the congregation have any source of new inputs into its patterns of life? Small churches are organized to live within recurrent patterns. That is normal. But the creative God is always calling us onward. When new inputs arise are they resisted? Or are they evaluated and incorporated? When new members join are their traditions respected or rejected? When an unexpected event happens does the congregation seek God's hand in the midst of it? Are changes in the environment welcomed as God's invitation?

4. *Connections to environment*. An unhealthy congregation walls itself in a bastion of self-righteousness and defensiveness. In that "safe" place it cannot be affected by events outside of itself. But neither can God's call to move on be heard. Healthy congregations are open to God's voice in both internal prophecy and external need. Jesus dined with publicans and sinners. Does the congregation ever connect with real, live sinners? Are there any links to those outside of the congregation?

Let me tell you a tale of two churches. Both were involved in a pastoral search. Both were asked by the judicatory minister to identify the image of the church held by neighbors and strangers. One was so disconnected from its neighbors and strangers that it could only think to ask pastors in the local clergy group. Two years later this congregation is smaller and weaker still. The other congregation asked everyone it could and discovered that nobody had a clue who or where the church was. So it set about increasing its visibility: rock concerts on the lawn, a daycare center, publicity in the local paper, everything they could think of. Today this church is a role model for congregational health!

5. *Story*. Can a central spiritual story be discerned? A spiritual story is often expressed in the recounting of the congregation's founding. Sometimes it emerges in the account of the congregation's victory over a particular trauma, such as a fire. Sometimes it is carried in the memory of certain saints now departed. If the story tells the history of the congregation's response to God's call in an inspiring and formative way, it can contribute greatly to congregational health.

6. *Myths and metaphors*. What underlying themes and filters at work in the congregation shape its life and ideas for the future? What metaphors provide a launching pad or a glass ceiling? For example, does the

congregation think of itself as the little engine that could or as the cartoon figure with a black cloud constantly over his head?

7. *Spiritual integration.* How do individual members integrate faith with daily life? Do congregants expect to be informed or challenged on Sunday about Monday-through-Friday matters? Or is religion a "parallel universe" that never intersects daily life?

8. *Divine future.* Where is God relative to the congregation's image of the future? Is it on its way to the promised land? Or in permanent exile, forgotten by God? Does it constantly pine for a lost Eden? Or merrily march to Zion?

9. *Challenges.* When challenged, how does the congregation respond? Does it wilt or bristle? Or is it energized? Can the congregation discern which challenges to tackle? Does it see challenges as spiritually threatening or as God's call to growth and learning?

10. *Happiness.* Is the joy of the Lord evident? Or is doom and gloom the normative emotion?

Of course, no small church will get an A+ on each of these tests of spiritual vitality. Nevertheless, these indicators can provide a means of assessing a congregation's spiritual health and help to determine an agenda for addressing areas of weakness.

CALLING

Does the congregation have a clear sense of history, identity, and hope? Do congregants know that the God who has gifted and used them in the past has a future in mind? I regularly use three exercises to help surface a congregation's sense of its past, present, and future in the will of God.

1. *The past, our history.* For the "Time Line" exercise I hang newsprint sheets on the walls. Each is labeled with a decade, going back to the birthdate of the eldest member and including the founding date and dates of any other major events. After a covered-dish supper, or a dessert or a luncheon, I ask parishioners to fill the sheets with their memories of that period. Who was the pastor? What was going on in the church? What ministries were happening? Who were some of the memorable characters in the church? What was the church's strength at that time? Its weakness?

And so on. (Note: There are many variations on this theme. Some like to use a separate sheet for each pastor's tenure. Some like to divide the sheets in half, noting the positives on one side and the negatives on the other. Some divide the sheets into thirds: the church, the community and the wider world/ society.) After the data has been written the congregation is then invited to identify any themes that run through the years. From this a sense of calling ("We are the church that . . .") and many core values can often be discerned.

2. *The present, our identity.* For the "Shield" exercise I hand each member a drawing of a crest divided into four areas:

"Shield"

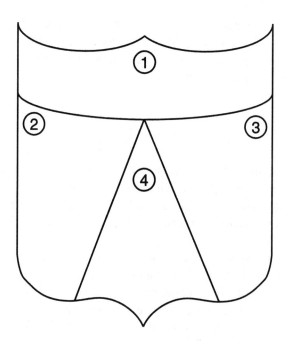

Members are to place in each area a picture, word, or phrase that answers the question of that area of the crest. These questions are (1) What do we hold most dear? (2) What are our greatest strengths? (3) What are our greatest opportunities? (4) What symbol(s) depicts the special or unique nature of this congregation?

After each person has had a chance to fill in the shields, we share our responses with the whole group. (In a larger church this sharing might take place in subgroups.) The answers are combined onto a large shield that can be displayed in the church, thus helping to reinforce the particular identity of the congregation.

3. *The future, our hopes.* For the "Award" exercise I invite members to divide into groups of four. I then announce that the year is 20xx (five years hence) and that the denomination is giving them the "Congregation of the Year" award. In their groups I ask them to list why they have won this award. Then I bring them together to share their reasons. These I list on newsprint sheets at the front of the room. Then we group the various items by theme to create a tangible expression of the aspirations and hopes of the congregation.

These exercises help the congregation to evaluate itself and to identify areas of greater and lesser health. Together these exercises yield a sense of the continuity of faithfulness in the congregation from the past, through the present, and into the future.

COMMON LIFE

Almost every society of humans that continues over time has a healthy common life. Relatively healthy, that is. Yet there are six common illnesses— the six pitfalls to health—that can prevent congregations, especially small-church congregations, from living in robust faith. These illnesses revolve around conflict, control, traditionalism, self-esteem, secrecy, and trauma. My primary purpose is to sensitize the reader to these six pitfalls. If a congregation falls into one (or more!) of these pitfalls, its life energy will be bled away. If diagnosed, however, efforts at increasing health can be more focused and effective.

1. *Conflict.* Conflict can either be very positive or very negative in the life of a congregation. Conflict is positive when it focuses attention on

issues that matter, invites different responses, allows new solutions, widens the group of "winners," and heightens sensitivity to God's will. Conflict is negative when it escalates out of control, when the rules of conflict are themselves destructive, and when it is so pervasive that it paralyzes the congregation. Conflict that solves a problem or allows a win-win solution is within the range of health. But when it requires camps, when it requires the other camp to lose, leave, or be destroyed, conflict is unhealthy. Rules of conflict can themselves be healthy or unhealthy. "Fighting fair" includes such things as owning emotions, speaking up, communicating directly, avoiding all-or-nothing thinking, and active listening. "Fighting dirty" involves forming camps, acting out, speaking behind others' backs, and harboring grudges. When unhealthy ways of handling conflict become the congregation's norm for behavior, a serious situation exists.

2. *Control.* A healthy congregation will share power, have a situational approach to authority, be respectful but not cowered of its leaders, cultivate and support new leaders, and take itself lightly, realizing that God is ultimately in charge! Unhealthy congregations do the opposite. The following questions can help determine whether a congregation is at risk of falling into the control pitfall. How soon are new members allowed into key leadership positions? Do the matriarchs and patriarchs seek out and equip apprentices? How large a fraction of the membership has areas of authority? Can any one person or family unilaterally block a desired change?

3. *Traditionalism.* Small churches are traditional. This can be a healthy reality. After all, when our heritage is known and honored our identity is strengthened. Tradition*ism*, however, is an unhealthy way to relate to the past. Traditionalism dictates that nothing can change. Things must stay the way they are. Traditionalism compulsively holds onto the forms of the past while forgetting or ignoring the dynamic spirit that constructed those forms. Traditionalism prays to the God who was helpful in ages past but opposes the God who is the hope for years to come. Tradition is the foundation upon which we can move faithfully into God's future. Traditionalism is a jail that denies the possibility of God's tomorrow. Tradition enhances life. Traditionalism is a form of premature death.

4. *Self-Esteem.* Believe it or not, it is possible for a congregation to have too high a level of self-esteem. A few of my congregations are "churches with an attitude," as I call them. In one case the congregation is living on its reputation and has an inflated self-image. In another case the congregation is strong and vibrant and knows it all too well. The more prominent pitfall of

self-esteem, however, particularly among small churches, is low self-esteem. "We're no good." "What happened to the 'good old days'?" "We don't offer anything for young families." "Who would want to join us?" Such negative self-assessment is contagious. It spreads within the congregation. And it spreads to most visitors. Thus it becomes a self-fulfilling prophecy. Just as individuals who have not integrated into their souls the good news that God loves them unconditionally and that they are worthwhile have not achieved a full measure of spiritual health, so it is with a church. Congregations are the Body of Christ, God's creation. We attribute worth first theologically and then in practical terms.

5. *Secrecy*. Like many people, many congregations deal with bad news by containing it and then hiding it. Over time this compounds the original problem. We are meant to live in the light. Secrecy inhibits and then paralyzes. In one of my churches the pastor agreed to leave abruptly after he was charged with an ethical violation. The deacons handled the matter and, seeking to "protect" the rest of the folks, kept the reasons and the process absolutely hush-hush. One Sunday the pastor was in the pulpit, the next he was gone and the parsonage was completely emptied out. A year later the interim pastor called me for help, citing conflict, a low level of trust, and "stuckness." When we were finally able to initiate a process that unmasked the secret, the congregation was able to move forward. Signs that secrecy is at work are contained in such comments as: "I never know what's going on around here," "They make all the decisions and we are lucky to find out later," and "Keep this in the strictest confidence." Avoidance of certain obvious realities can also indicate a collusion of silence. Snide comments, oblique allusions, chatter at the social periphery—all may indicate that there is an "elephant in the living room," so to speak. Secrets freeze up a congregation. Naming them in love is real and challenging ministry.

6. *Trauma*. Like secrecy, trauma can paralyze a congregation. The fire that destroyed the building of one of my congregations has held them captive for more than a decade. The historic building, the beautiful stained glass, the site of a century of memories—all were gone in a couple of hours. The congregation immediately rebuilt a more modest structure on the site, but parishioners never quite made it their home. In some ways the congregation is made up of two groups: those who remember the old building and grieve, and those, mostly newcomers, who want to get on with being a church. Needless to say, the latter group is frustrated! Trauma cannot be wished away, but the congregation will not achieve a solid degree of health unless it grieves, heals, and then releases.

Mission

What is God calling us to do in the community in the service of the kingdom? Where do the passion of the congregation and the opportunities in its context intersect? Just as Christ came not to be served but to serve, no Body of Christ is healthy if its exclusive concern is its own well-being. A Christian congregation is only healthy when it is serving, giving, caring, and involved in needs outside of itself. The specific service is less important then the involvement beyond its own threshold. Evangelism, advocacy, and social action are particulars of the Spirit's impulse to minister. You know the difference between the life-filled Sea of Galilee and the lifeless Dead Sea. The former has an outlet while the Dead Sea only takes in!

I believe that every healthy congregation has received from the Spirit a passion about something beyond itself. And I firmly believe that every congregation has been equipped and gifted by the Spirit in particular ways. The church that has learned to apply its gifts in service of its divine calling is living in God-ordained health. The church that denies its giftedness and squelches its passion has collapsed in on itself. The size of the enterprise is not the issue; doing mission is.

I know of one small church that does not have enough bodies, energy, and resources to do ongoing programs of mission. But parishioners felt the need to reach out in some way. So they offered themselves up as the annual coordinators for their county CROP Walk (an ecumenical fundraising program for hunger relief). They do just that one thing, but they do it with joy and enthusiasm and so serve their needy neighbors and others across the globe.

An exercise to help assess a congregation's missionary health is as follows. Post two sheets of newsprint on a central wall. Title the first "WE ARE . . ." Invite parishioners to describe themselves, for example, we are loving, steady, survivors, and so on. Title the second "WE DO . . ." and draw a vertical line down the middle. As parishioners suggest various items, record what the congregation does for itself on one side and what it does for others on the other. Lead a discussion of the relative balance between the two sides. (Often in small churches current activities can be adapted easily to move from the "for us" side to the "for others" side. For example, a covered-dish supper for fellowship could be adapted for outreach by adding a community-oriented program and a bit of publicity.)

DEVELOPMENT OF LEADERSHIP

The final area of congregational health that we will consider here is the development of leadership. Leadership is a critical dynamic in any size church, but the small church may be especially vulnerable to the effects of ill health in this area. A large church may recognize its need for a wide, diverse, and ongoing stream of leaders. In the small church sharing leadership may be seen as threatening. What is the attitude of leadership in the congregation toward potential leaders? Are they supportive and empowering? Or do they hoard their power and undermine others? A healthy small church will build a pool of leaders-to-be. An unhealthy congregation will clutch leadership tightly.

Another dimension of health in this area concerns the level of inclusion. What proportion of new persons have been let into the leadership ranks? I led a leadership retreat at one of my churches a few years ago. Thirty people were in attendance, but when I asked how many had less than five years' tenure three people raised their hands. A 2 percent annual transition in leadership is not the mark of a dynamic and growing congregation!

A third dimension of health in the area of leadership has to do with the patterns of inclusion into the leadership ranks. Do people become leaders with little or no training? Or do current leaders seek out apprentices, involving them with encouragement and love? Does the congregation look for new ways to involve people in leadership, creating new niches based on their gifts and passions?

Finally let us inquire if the leadership is growing in spirit, skill, and ability. Is "leadership" equated only with work, therefore leading to burnout? Or are leaders growing in spirit and ability? Is there a sense of excitement and joy among leaders? Or does duty and resignation prevail? Is training offered for different leadership roles? Are retreats and/or celebrations part of the rewards of leadership or is it work only?

A SMALL-CHURCH HEALTH ASSESSMENT TOOL

Here is a quick, easy way to gain an insight into your small church's level of health and balance. The following six functions are described using explicitly tribal dynamics. Together they can yield a picture of the degree of health and balance in your small church.

1. *The Orientating Ritual.* "I hate it when I am sick and can't worship. My whole week seems off balance." Thus a long-time church member described the orienting power of regular worship. To function well in life we each need to be connected to greater realities. Corporations expend a lot of energy focusing company goals and then rationally aligning each employee's role with them. In the small church, however, it is not rationality but ritual that orients us in our world. Habit, tradition, and ceremony give us our place in God's universe. The regularity of worship renews our spiritual world. It reaffirms that God is sovereign. It helps us to remember that we live and move and dwell in divine love. The healthy small church uses this orientation for wholeness, faithfulness, obedience, and well-being. Are the rituals of your church orienting or disorienting? Are rituals used to orient worshipers to God's presence and vocation? Are elements of God's life, such as spontaneity, humor, correction, and calling, made to be comfortable and familiar? To what degree are the rituals in your church orienting in their human effect and God-focused in their direction?

2. *The Celebrative Feast.* The power of the shared meal has been known from time immemorial: Abraham entertained angels with food and drink. Jesus shared his last moments over a meal. The Pilgrims gave thanks with a big feast. Nothing builds and maintains the bonds between human beings more than eating together. The joy and the love, the thanksgiving and the celebration that God intended for us to enjoy as human beings finds a powerful expression in the shared meal. The irrepressible covered-dish supper gives testimony to this dynamic. Something socially and spiritually healthy happens when we break bread together. In what ways—desserts, coffee hours, covered-dish suppers—does your congregation share food?

3. *The Forming Campfire.* Since Christian faith is caught more than it is taught, we must provide the occasions when infectious Christians can be exposed to those younger in the faith. So the Spirit of God may be passed on to the upcoming generation. A tribe uses time around the campfire to tell those stories that make up its history and give substance to its identity.

So, too, the small church must create opportunities to pass on its spiritual traditions. A church without shared memories will soon be a church without direction and purpose. In what ways does the life of your congregation embody the campfire?

4. *The Caring Barn-Raising.* A healthy in a small church has ways of demonstrating love when the structures of life of an individual or family need to be rebuilt. The Amish, for example, come together as a community to erect a barn for one of its members when the previous barn has been destroyed. Small churches also rally around ailing members and help them to rebuild the damaged portions of their lives. One of my churches has a particular knack for embodying Christ's love toward people in special need of care. Tears welled in my eyes as I listened to a young single mother give testimony to Christ's love through the members of her small church. She believes they literally saved her life. When her marriage collapsed and her life seemed to be closing down around her, the love shown by this congregation replaced her despair with hope. In what ways does your congregation make real Christ's healing love?

5. *The Cooperative Hunt.* Just as a healthy small church will rally to meet the needs of its members, so, too, will it band together to accomplish an objective necessary for its health and ministry. Often this requires the cooperative efforts of every member of the group. I am fascinated by filmed accounts of aboriginal tribes tracking down and killing a lion or wild boar. It is thrilling to watch these marginally nourished people with flimsy hand-made weapons, by coordinated effort and with sheer pluck and faith, bring down an animal that could have easily destroyed any one of them, and so provide the tribe with food or protect it from danger. Small-church members, too, can accomplish great things when they work together. One of my congregations decided to get its light out from under the bushel when members divided up the phonebook and called every family to invite them to worship. Even though they had moved out of a storefront into their own building only months before, they are now finding their new space too small for all of those responding! What efforts at outreach has your congregation committed itself to?

6. *Trusted Elders.* Tribes seldom vote on the decision before them or elect members to represent them. Rather, tribes function by investing particular members with authority in certain areas. These members are thus given the status of elder and justify the trust of the tribe by responsibly exercising their authority. How does a small church allocate the tasks

necessary to secure its faithfulness and health? In many churches officers and board members are elected to execute the jobs specified in the bylaws. After their term, usually three years, they retire or go on to another job. In the small church tasks are allocated by trust after competence has been demonstrated. Individuals are invested with authority because the congregation recognizes in them a God-given ability. Of course, this system breaks down when trust or trustworthiness is in short supply, or when someone dependable in one area wants to control other areas as well. Does your congregation trust and empower its members for service to God on behalf of the whole?

The following graph (page 109) can be used to help a small church assess its health and balance. This tool can be administered at a leaders' meeting, or after a covered-dish supper, and so on. The graph is fun to use, and the process will reveal as much about the logic of church members as they place their various activities on the graph as it will reveal about the placement itself.

Measures of Small-Church Health

	The Orientating Ritual	The Celebrative Feast	The Forming Campfire	The Caring Barn-Raising	The Cooperative Hunt	Trusted Elders	Church Activity
a.							
b.							
c.							
d.							
e.							
f.							
g.							
h.							
i.							
j.							
k.							

Ask the group to make a list of everything the congregation does. This may take up several newsprint sheets. Then go back through the list and mark the tribal function that each activity falls into. (Note: one activity may be listed under more than one function.) Rewrite the list under the appropriate tribal functions. As a group, assess whether or not the activities of the church seem adequate in each function, and whether or not the congregation's overall energy is fairly well balanced. For example, one worship service a week may be adequate, but three "campfires" (for instance, Bible study or heritage event) may not if a certain group (for example, seniors who don't drive at night) is unable to attend any of them. If the congregation considers itself weak in a particular function (as is often the case with "the hunt"), try to come up with new activities or consider adapting existing activities in some way to serve this function.

One of my congregations realized that the use of contemporary music and instruments was making worship disorienting for many long-term members, and it wasn't attracting new people to Sunday morning either. So, in the spirit of "the hunt," congregants reconceptualized the contemporary elements and moved them to a more viable time.

Conclusion

Assessing congregational health is an ongoing quest. It is good to do, but obsessing over it is never helpful. The assessment tools presented in this chapter are not perfect, certainly, but as indicators of congregational health they can provide enough insight to evaluate the degree of congregational health and perhaps identify the issues to address in the future life of your church. There is as much art as there is science in assessing congregational health. These tools are intended to complement the personal maturity, common sense, spiritual depth, and presence of the Spirit that all effective small-church leaders bring to the ministry.

CHAPTER NINE

Leadership Activities in the Small-Church World

"Be doers of the Word, and not hearers only." (James 1:2)

How can we act, then, as small-church lovers and leaders? Numerous leadership strategies are consistent with the nature of the small church. As you become more cognizant of the social dynamics in small congregations, you will undoubtedly create and develop your own strategies. But if you are not quite at that point, this chapter and the next present leadership activities to help you get started. Utilize them, mix and match, or let them kindle your strategic imagination!

DO, THEN DISCUSS!

"Plan the work and work the plan." So the pastor of a medium-sized, suburban church advised me during my seminary field placement. Very wise advice, too. Of course, it is based on the assumption that effort flows from intention. This it did in his parish: long-range planning committees led to new building plans that, in turn, led to new buildings.

But the flow, if there is one, is usually the other way in the small church: behavior leads to its own justification. Leadership in the small church is an exercise not in rationality but in rationale. Behaviors that are sustained over time in the life of the congregation justify themselves by their very presence. Actions are right if we do them and have done them for time-out-of-mind. At least they're right for us.

A story is told of a small-church pastor who wanted to introduce a change in the way communion was observed. From the board he requested a six-month trial period for the new ceremony. Apparently feeling that this was too brief a period to cause any real harm, the board approved the request. After the trial period was over, the pastor, very conscientiously, asked the board members if they would like to stick with the new ritual. "Huh? What new ceremony? That's the way we've always done it. What else is on your mind, Pastor?" Had they really forgotten their old ceremony? Who knows? They were using their memories in service of their identity, not the facts. So harmonious was the new ceremony with their common life that it felt as though it had always been with them. "We've always done it that way" is just another way of saying, "It is us." Behavior had led to rationale and acceptance in a way a rational discussion never could. Or put another way, for small-church people theology explains praxis. But the praxis is the important thing. For a change of behavior to be accepted and incorporated in a small church, it must be experienced. It may be rejected after it is experienced, but it will almost certainly be rejected if the only apprehension of it is theoretical.

What does this mean for small-church leaders? It means that it is by doing, not by discussing, that small-church people decide about the helpfulness and faithfulness of changes. Small-church leaders may employ two strategies to pave the way for the doing: trial periods and increments. Trial periods, as noted above, reduce the threat of the doing. It is like trying on a hat: if it doesn't fit, it is OK to put it back on the shelf. Increments allow people to get into a new behavior step by step. I presented these action strategies at a workshop. When I finished, one lady let out a sigh. "I'm so concerned about the teenagers in our town," she said. "Many are into drugs, in part because they have nothing else to do. But when I proposed that the trustees open up the church for a Saturday night dance, I was turned down flat. How can they be so un-Christian?"

It was obvious to me that this lady really cared. "Instead of lamenting their faithlessness, let's consider the situation's dynamics from a folk-society perspective," I said.

> You were asking to introduce a change into the pattern of the church. Change, including discussion thereof, activates fear in the hearts of folk people. Some were probably afraid the building would be misused. Some were afraid of this "perverse and untoward generation." Some may have been brought up to view dancing as of the devil. Some may just fear anything different. All these fears,

and more, you probably activated by asking for the whole thing at once. My hunch is that few small-church people like being pushed into the deep end of the pool. Most stick a toe in, take a step or two in, and then wade in backward! And who is to say that a dance would have interested the kids you are concerned about? Why not take it a step at a time. Ask for an OK for you and a few kids to use the hall a couple of nights for Monopoly, or whatever, maybe as a part of your youth group program. No drugs. No dancing. You'll clean up. No threat. Just a little more of what we're already doing. If it catches on, build it up and invite a trustee each night to help out. If not, you're no worse off than you are with the 'No' you've got now.

I could almost see the light bulb go on in her head!

GO BACK TO THE FUTURE

For those of us trained in the ways of modernity, it seems that the past, including tradition, heritage, and "the way we've always done it," is an enemy, maybe the enemy, or at best unnecessary baggage weighing down every forward step. How much more appropriate it would be for us, especially we who name the name of the One who lived two thousand years ago, we who look for guidance in a book started three millennia ago, to see the past as an ally, a means of moving into God's future. The past can provide the grist for moving forward in terms of insight, inspiration, and identity. I would like to tell you about my own journey on this road.

Early in my pastorate I felt myself at a decision point not of my own making. Denomination officials, my parents, even some parishioners were all sending me a message: a good pastor doesn't stay in a small church for long; he pays his dues and then takes a step up the ladder. I felt torn between a conscious desire to succeed and an unconscious desire to stay put and minister, to "progress" not by moving out but by sticking it out. As the intensity of this struggle began to increase within my soul, I happened upon the book *Small Churches Are Beautiful*.[1] One of the first essays describes the pastoral situation of colonial New England. I was fascinated and stirred by what I learned. In the past, pastoral status was lodged in one's calling to the ministry, not in the quantitative indices of one's parish.

The rural small-church pastor and the urban large-church pastor stood on equal ground. In part this was so because pastorates were long—usually a lifetime! Nearly 80 percent of colonial pastors served one church all their lives. And the 5 percent or so who had more than two were considered ne'er-do-wells, either troublemakers or bereft of the qualities of perseverance and fortitude.

In that moment of "relearning" my past I gained a tremendous insight into my value framework. I had been basing my self-esteem as a pastor on a twentieth-century business model. From the past I was liberated to accept another model, a model based on quality, calling, loyalty, and historical precedent. In that moment I was freed from the debilitation of my internal conflict. I was freed to serve my parish with renewed energy. Many years have passed since then and I am still amazed at how far forward I have come because I looked backward. History. Insight. Energy. Ministry.

During a visit to a parish family, they casually mentioned a booklet published by the Block Island Historical Society. "Which is that?" I asked. "Haven't read it? Here, take this extra copy." I did. And my attitude toward my parish and the congregation's attitude toward themselves have never been the same since. Previously I had read some history of the island, but the origins of the church seemed lost in the mist of time. It had taken the white settlers over a century to get around to founding a church, and even then history records mostly construction details. It didn't sound very inspiring. But then I read the booklet *The Real Mystery of Block Island*,[2] by Arthur Kinoy, an attorney. Reasoning like a trial lawyer and weaving facts, logic, and psychology, Kinoy paints a picture of a struggling band of people of conscience meeting secretly behind closed doors in Boston just after the public lynching of Mary Dyer. They were bound together by a quest for religious freedom. Against major odds and forsaking their business interests, wealth, and social position, they landed on the shores of little Block Island following the siren of liberty. Led by Captain Sands in civic affairs, Simon Ray in spiritual matters, and Trustrum Dodge in the practical aspects of wresting life from a hostile environment, they established not just a viable settlement but a community of faith based on "soul liberty" and individual conscience.

For nearly a hundred years, Kinoy writes, Ray and his son Simon Jr. led home worship, feeding the souls of those daring families, nourishing them in the fight for liberty. By the year Simon Ray Jr. passed on, the forces for national political liberty were on a collision course with England, and the forces were well established, too, which would result in the Bill of Rights. Yes, the settling of Block Island was only a tiny thread, but it was a thread in the great tapestry of freedom. So was I, pastor in the succession of men and women who risked all for their conscience and their God. My congregation worshiped and ministered in the succession of those who forged freedom. To us they had passed the torch. I would hold it high. What an honor and an inspiration to be their spiritual descendants. History. Inspiration. Energy. Mission.

Outside it was a cold, early spring evening. But it was warm inside as a couple of dozen members of the church gathered to share a covered-dish supper and afterward learn about the fire that destroyed the previous church building. The meal was good, and we were all mellow, jovial, and no more focused than ever as we started talking about the fire of December 3, 1944. Why hadn't we rebuilt there? How many buildings had we had over the years? Five? Where were they? One thing led to another until finally the facts emerged. We'd had five church buildings, the previous four having burned to the ground, and not once had the new building been built on the previous site. Why not? Quarrels with neighbors, ha ha? Maybe we had never owned the land!

Then slowly it dawned on us. The first building built in the late 1700s was on the site of the original settlement. Decades later the town hall and grinding mills were built nearer to the fishing harbors, so there the church relocated after fire razed the first building. Half a century later the breakwater was finished, making the first permanent harbor. So there was the church rebuilt when fire struck again. And so on. Every church building had been erected in the center of the social life of our community. In the history of our buildings we came to understand not only who we were as a congregation but also who we had always been. We were the church, in location and in mission, which was in touch with the center of community life. That one realization reconfirmed our self-understanding, set it in the context of centuries, and motivated us to be who we were. In our history we had found our identity clarified. History. Identity. Energy. Mission.

The heritage of the parish can also provide a lever for moving forward in faithfulness and ministry. David Ray, small-church pastor and author of *Small Churches Are the Right Size*,[3] tells of the time his former parishioners in Warwick, Massachusetts, literally rummaged around in the attic of their "house" church (their church building was an old colonial house). The congregation was in the midst of debating whether to add a sanctuary wing with room for Sunday School classes and community activities. Then, Deuteronomy-like, the documents regarding acquisition of the original building were discovered. It was found that behind the purchase of the house decades earlier had been the intention to use it, not only for worship but, especially, to service the community. This truth from their past gave precedent and therefore legitimacy to their present concern to build for more effective ministry to the community. So build they did.

Some of the most effective leadership acts small-church pastors can perform are to become history buffs, read up on the struggle of faith of the parish, sit at the feet of some of the elder members, and play "remember when . . ." Initially this may seem like wasted time to a young, energetic, ambitious pastor, but in reality it is time well spent. It will provide the pieces of the puzzle that can be assembled at the point at which God calls the congregation forward.

Effective small-church leaders will not use bold, pie-in-the-sky visions of the New Jerusalem, or babble on about a bright new tomorrow. They will speak quietly about who we are on the basis of who we always have been, about how we can become even more of who we are, about what was good about the "good old days," and about how we can keep that good alive in our midst today.

PUT A FACE ON IT

In the basement of a small church in Hope, Rhode Island, there was a scale model of a well, complete with roof and bucket. It was labeled "Ronnie's Well" and within the well opening were many coins and bills. My curiosity aroused, I inquired, "What's this?" "Oh," came the reply. "The Peace Corps has a project to dig wells to provide usable water for certain villages in a remote section of Africa where water is scarce. So far we've raised hundreds of dollars through collections and projects to help buy the equipment needed for the wells." Well, that explained the model well and the money, but why was this small group of people so highly committed to a project halfway around the globe, a project and a need so remote that virtually no one had ever heard of it? "Oh, that's 'cause of Ronnie. He told us all about it." I was apparently more obtuse than usual that day because I still didn't get it. "Who's Ronnie?"

"Oh, Ronnie is a young man," they answered, "who grew up in our church. His family is very active. After college he wanted to do something for others so he joined the Peace Corps. His assignment was these wells. He wrote us letters and sent pictures explaining his work. You could just sense how important it was to him and the people in the villages to get these wells working. So we've been sending him as much money as we can raise ever since. We think God is really using Ronnie." My heart warmed once I grasped what it was all about.

That evening I reflected on the little model well with the money tucked into it. The need was there with or without the Peace Corps. The Peace Corps was there with or without Ronnie. Yet could I imagine a small church responding to such a need without the Ronnie connection? I couldn't. There are thousands of Third World villages across our globe with needs as compelling, but how many churches work so hard to minister to even one of them? What would a pastor or mission encourager have to do to actualize such a response? I could barely conceive of a scenario apart from a Ronnie.

What did Ronnie do for that small group of Christians, struggling to keep the church doors open themselves, which released compassion and caring, effort and resources? Ronnie put a face on the need. He personalized it. No longer were the villagers faceless unknowns. They were people named and described, and so obviously cared about by Ronnie. The parishioners cared about Ronnie. Ronnie cared about the villagers. Therefore the parishioners cared about the villagers. Ronnie brought them into the tribe; Ronnie appealed to the church's covenantal bonds. There was no anticipation of quid pro quo. The good Christians of Hope were doing what was right to do. They were caring for their own. Ronnie, by his life and love, had made a village halfway around the world a part of the relational network of that small church.

The typical small church will not respond except perfunctorily to impersonal, data-fied, remote needs. To them mission begins and ends at home. By this I mean that needs which have a claim on us to respond are perceived as personal, actual, close at hand, a disruption in the well-being of the community. This is what motivates a response, not abstract, theoretical, remote, and statistically defined needs.

Churches with a "global consciousness" may be able to motivate response on the basis of the objective extent of human need across the world. Churches with "tribal-consciousness" are very seldom able to do so. Here a different strategy must be employed. Rather than bring the church into the need, the need must be brought into the church. Effective small-church leaders will find ways to put a face on the needs to which God is calling the church to respond. This must be done with care. People's feelings and dignity must not be sacrificed. But it is not impossible. After all, if a need has no face, whose need is it?

There are many ways to personalize need.

1. *Describe the situation in personal terms.* The deacons at Harbor Church were for years invited to contribute to a local shelter for homeless women but didn't respond. When they heard of the situation of two families helped by the shelter and others that the shelter could not afford to help, however, their hearts were touched.

2. *Establish relationships.* Go and visit. Or bring someone into the life of the congregation. Harbor Church's support of state Hispanic programs had been through formal channels and were uninspired. But when one of our parishioners worshiped with the Hispanic church and the pastor there, Francisco, chatted with us over a covered-dish supper, our people immediately started coming up with ways to help. The number of unemployed Hispanics in the state was a sad statistic to which we had no idea how to respond. But we knew how to befriend people. Francisco was now our friend. We were pleased to stand behind him, hear news of his work, and support his ministry as we could.

3. *Start at home.* "Mission begins at home" can be an excuse to do little or nothing. But what's wrong with inviting people to put their money where their mouth is? Isn't it better than lamenting the lack of global concern and so doing nothing at all? Find out who's hurting in the church. Who needs a job, a minor repair, money for medicine, a personal visit? A group from a Presbyterian church in Pennsylvania working with the Habitat for Humanity program asked if they could do home repairs for the elderly and/or impoverished on Block Island. I didn't know, but I would find out. A deacon and I visited ten homes, asking permission and looking for needs. And we found 'em! My eyes were opened to the needs right on my doorstep. Right away our churchmen started Helping Hands, a program to continue work on these necessary repairs.

4. *Expand horizons.* Once mission becomes a patterned behavior its object can be broadened. When I first arrived the Harbor Church congregation was very insular in outlook, especially regarding mission. The number of families who regularly contributed to the denominational mission program could be counted on one hand, with a couple fingers left over. The concern was solely for "our own." So we developed ways to further help

our own: the Mary D Fund (for energy assistance), Project Harvest Share (distributing excess garden produce to shut-ins), and the Second Wind Luncheons (for elderly companionship). Once mission activity became more comfortable it began to expand. A SERRV (a ministry of Church World Service that markets Third World handcrafts) table was started, which I was thrilled to hear had over $1,000 in sales one year, and then half a dozen people started talking about a mission trip to a church a few towns away to help out with a building repair project! Previously unimaginable behavior. But as we got into mission, mission got into us.

Arrange an "Accident"

One of the characteristics of folkways is that no one knows who originated them. They just happened. There is something "right" about them: what we do is in the order of things; it was not invented by someone. A preplanned, rational program, proposed and promoted by the pastor or other upstart, is seldom incorporated directly into the life of the tribe. In the face of this dynamic, how can small-church leaders proceed? A shift in focus is required. We must move away from the logical and rational approach and let life provide the impetus to faithfulness.

I once heard of a family who lived by the side of the river. Their existence was one of material marginality but spiritual surfeit. They gardened and gathered firewood, but primarily they looked to the river, not to find a way over it but to capture the "stuff" of life floating downstream for their use and benefit. I submit that the reason we don't "mine" life is a weakness of faith, and a limitation of vision. We feel more in control if we are planning and programming. But control and faithfulness are not the same. Life's interruptions are filled with God's intentions. John Hostetler, in his interesting book *Amish Society*,[4] describes the effects of two "accidents" on the understanding and behavior of the closed Amish society.

> Chance, or what might be called accidental happenings, also have the effect of altering traditional behavior patterns. In Ohio, two young robbers whose vehicle was stalled in a ditch entered a farmhouse home after dark on the evening of July 18, 1957, and in the course of events shot the father, Amishman Paul Coblentz. One of the young men, Cleo Peters, was given the death sentence.

Many Amish people signed petitions urging mercy. Nine hours before he was scheduled to die, Governor William O'Neill commuted the sentence to life imprisonment. Some Amish people "became burdened about the spiritual welfare" of Cleo Peters. They wrote letters to him and also sent delegations to visit him. Discussions and correspondence followed the conversion of Mr. Peters. The sad incident was interpreted as an act of God, as stated in a letter to the prisoner: "We believe that God allowed this to call us back to Him in the work of winning souls to His kingdom.". . .

An escaped convict in the Midwest was discovered working as an Amish farmhand. Without knowing that he was a convict, the Amish befriended him and prepared to receive him into their church by baptism. At this time he confessed his status. Shortly before baptism, someone reported him to the law officers, who arrested him. He was returned to prison in the state where he had been convicted only to be paroled. Members of the Amish church met him as he left the prison and took him to their community. . . .

Such unstructured incidents, drawn from widely differing communities, have the effect of evoking new sentiments or concerns for the outsider. They force the traditional community into thinking on new courses of action. When taken as "acts of God," new courses of action, which would otherwise be resented, are made legitimate.

What could have independently moved the typically xenophobic Amish culture to befriend and convert an imprisoned murderer? I can conceive of no plan or program that could accomplish that. Yet it occurred. Not only did it occur, but it was interpreted as God's call back to their true selves!

What cannot be planned can be envisioned and orchestrated for God's kingdom. At one point at Harbor Church, I was tired of living and worshiping (the sanctuary and parsonage are in the same building) in a century-old, drafty, uninsulated, code-violating, rundown building. But meeting general expenses was a struggle. How could we ever get the vision to repair and renovate our facility? As I mulled over these issues, I got the bill for the church's previous load of fuel oil. It had been one of the coldest years in recent memory. By the last week of December we were way over budget for heating oil already. Yet another bill could very well have broken us. I could sit on it a week, creating the illusion of fiscal solvency by deferring the expense to the next year, or I could look for the blessing, seeing the bill as an instrument of God. The extremely cold year, was it accidental or providential?

I asked the treasurer to pay the bill immediately. At our annual business meeting two weeks later the people were shocked by our oil overage. I asked for a committee to investigate installing new windows and insulation. Motion passed without dissent. Six months of homework later, the committee proposed a complete renovation and had $23,000 pledged to start us off! It took five years of blood, sweat, and tears, but our church building was eventually renovated and up to code. That one unplanned, oversized fuel bill moved us as no rational argument could have. An "accident" always motivates a folk society more than an argument.

CREATE A CADRE

Sometimes the best way to get something done is not to try to get anything done. This approach is, of course, nonsense to those who have bought into the values of corporate America. What good is someone who doesn't aim at getting anything done? For these people, doers are actors and the world around them is acted upon. It is a little more intricate for the Christian, though. In the Christian world God is the actor and the world evidences God's actions. We are to discern God's activity and coordinate ourselves with it. It is still more intricate in the folk society. Leadership activity is likely to be resisted, as Moses found out: "Who appointed *you* lord and master over *us*?"

I distinctly remember being burned by this latter dynamic. I was the spokesperson for a town-appointed committee on Block Island. We had done an incredible amount of homework, marshaled our data and arguments, and attempted to persuade our town fathers to budget for improved medical service in the upcoming fiscal year. I presented a case that was thoroughly convincing, at least to me. But instead of unanimous support our committee was raked over the coals! Finally the town fathers decided to defer the decision. I was stunned. Next the town road worker submitted his budget request. "Do you want us to approve this increase?" A shrug. "Whatever you'd like to do." "Do you really need this much money?" "Nope. Only if you want the roads tended." "Why should we pass this now?" "So I can go home and watch the rest of the Red Sox game."

Request approved! A townsperson, noticing my dazed look, took pity on me. "You know where you went wrong, Reverend? You acted like you really wanted your request approved. You shudda played it cool like John. If they think you're pushing, they wonder what you're trying to put over on them." This dynamic is operative in the small church, too. To get too intense about one's agenda is to inhibit, not increase, the likelihood of the desired outcome.

Thus it is sometimes better to do nothing. I think this was the real genius of the Men's Prayer Breakfast. We had no explicit agenda, except to share and pray. As we got more comfortable (realized that no one was going to shove his agenda down another's throat), the level of sharing deepened. As the sharing deepened, personal and churchwide concerns began to be voiced and clarified. As we became more sensitive to our own needs, we discerned those we could do something about. Out of that realization came ministry. Not necessarily a ministry I would have chosen, but the right one nonetheless. Our outreach emerged not out of any planning, not out of "being intentional," not out of any goal setting, but out of what God had put in our hearts.

In folk societies generational kinship is complemented by a secondary but important social structure. In certain cultures it is defined by gender, in others it is bracketed by age, in others it is like a club with strict rules. These associations play a crucial role in the life of the tribe. They accomplish certain specific functions or redress social imbalances. They have their own ministry, but they are structured for form, not function. The energy released in such subgroups is an important factor for leadership. Wesley structured this in "class meetings." Duncan McIntosh talks about creating "hot spots" for change—a handful of like-minded people within the whole congregation. Paul Cho champions "cell groups." The power released when people get together to pray, share, and "just be" is tremendous, if not necessarily controllable. Effective small-church leaders will recognize that God is in control, we aren't. Gather some open-hearted folk and just see what God will do!

Summary

The action tools presented in this chapter are meant to facilitate the process of embodying God's calling in your situation. When brought to bear on the particulars of your situation they may help you realize God's intention by working with, not against, the social nature of the small church. Let us review them.

    1. *Do, then discuss!* The small church is primarily a reflexive entity, not a reflective one. It knows by experiencing, more than by analyzing. In doing, more than discussing, can a small church determine whether it is comfortable in proceeding. Effective small-church leaders allow experience as an input into important discussions. Two strategies that embody this dynamic are trial periods and increments.

    2. *Go back to the future.* Small churches are motivated more by their heritage than by a vision for the future. Effective small-church leaders become familiar with a church's heritage. We rummage around in the attic of the church's memories. This not only expands understanding, but it communicates a positive regard for our people. (It also gives small-church leaders leverage when action is required.) It allows the congregation its nature: to move forward by looking backward.

    3. *Put a face on it.* Small churches are motivated to respond to relational, not abstract, realities. Needs that are tangible, close at hand, personal, and within the relational network of the congregation can be registered and responded to. Four ways to move in this direction are to (1) describe issues in personal terms, (2) establish relationships, (3) start at home, and (4) expand horizons.

    4. *Arrange an "accident."* Small-church folk are more at home with fate than intentionality. We respond better to an "accident" than to an action plan. This may frustrate leaders who must have the church do their particular thing. But it works out fine for those who are looking to do God's thing! Effective small-church leaders take action cues from the particulars of the situation, and we know how to present them in a way that will catch the attention and energy of their congregations.

    5. *Create a cadre.* Few today consider prayer an action. Yet a handful of open, concerned Christians meeting to pray can catch fire and really brighten up their corner of the world. It was those few timid souls meeting behind closed doors upon whom the fire of the Holy Spirit fell. The world has not been the same since.

CHAPTER TEN

More Leadership Activities in the Small-Church World

If the preceding chapter has equipped you to function more effectively in your small church, you will be delighted to be able to add another set of strategies to your tool kit.

BE A CATALYST, NOT A CHAMPION

One pitfall I fell into as a younger pastor was the need to be the standard bearer. Certainly there are times when we are called to lead the charge, to crusade, to champion a cause. There are times, but they are not as frequent as we may think. We who have taken on leadership responsibilities in a local congregation, pastoral or lay, often do so because righteousness compels us. If there is a wrong, it needs be righted. A breach, it needs to be healed. An anguish, it needs to be comforted. A change, it needs to be implemented.

Well, now, here is where I would like to call us to slow down and think. Soldiers in the point position do not have a long life expectancy. Neither do we new pastors who appoint ourselves the standard bearers for change in our church. The change may be vitally needed, but that is not the operative issue. The real question is: Have we pastors built up enough trust and tenure to lead the charge? Often we pick up the flag out of our own need for significance or power, or even rigid theological rectitude. We might be better served to ask: To whom else has God given this task? How can I release and support this calling?

I now call such congregational crusaders "youngest sons." Consider the story of David in 1 Samuel 17. The Philistines have invaded Palestine and Saul has rallied Israel to oppose them. Apparently Saul marched at the

head of his troops until he saw Goliath. Then he realized the vulnerability of
that position. He throws the forward motion into neutral and the two armies
become stuck, Goliath threatening but not attacking, the Israelites quaking
but not retiring, and Saul wringing his hands. Then David appears. What do
we know about David? For one thing, he was the youngest son of Jesse.
Being a son put him squarely within the heritage of Israel, but being a youngest
son indicated his nature to be iconoclastic, rebellious, boastful, and noisy.
Youngest sons are often powerful agents for change because they tend to
color outside the lines, want to get their way, and can be charming to non-
relatives! Epitomizing this youngest-son identity, David soon finds himself
before King Saul volunteering to fight Goliath. What a godsend for Saul!
Yet he does something very interesting: he determines that David is indeed
a son of Israel (vv. 55-58). David is allowed to go against Goliath because
he is one of us (a son), and David wants to go because he is a youngest son.

Not long ago one of my congregations became stuck. Nearly three
decades ago the congregation had purchased a large lot upon which it was
going to build its dream sanctuary. Through bequests and the sale of the
parsonage the congregation had amassed almost $100,000 in the building
fund. But the congregation had dwindled down to a few dozen tired, discouraged folk. Although he was paid for only one day each week, the new
pastor began a number of new initiatives. But he didn't have the time to
bring them to completion. So he challenged congregants to rethink their
vision and invest in their present ministry. After all, he reasoned, what good
is a building fund, or even a brand-new building, if the congregation erodes
away to nothing? As logically and theologically valid as his arguments were,
they availed little. He had only been with the congregation a year and already he was challenging what its members held most sacred! It was a
formula for resistance, and the script played out. The pastor's frustration
mounted. And the people's intransigence solidified.

Into this impasse came the voice of one parishioner. A grandfather
himself, he was the son of two of the respected pillars of the church. He
had been called to supply the pulpit in a neighboring church, this one down
to a dozen elderly folk at worship. Preaching there week after week, he
came to see the future of his home church if nothing changed. Both publicly
and privately he began to champion the cause of new life now. He knew the
relational network and he used it. For decades of faithful service he had the
respect of the congregation. For his position as a son of pillars in the church
he was afforded a hearing. Two months later congregants met to decide

how to use the building fund. They chose to spend broke on full-time pastoring! Their willingness to decide and the boldness of their choice is due to the role played by their "youngest son."

Small churches move best from the inside. Thus, rather than be every cause's champion, it is far more effective to introduce change by finding the "youngest son" whom God has impassioned about a different future, supporting that call, and then releasing that person to minister within the relational network of communication and shared meaning.

TELL A TALE

Narrative is woven into the very fabric of tribal people. Story is at the heart of small-church life. We sing, "I love to tell the story" but then forget the primacy of storytelling in our small-church communication. We have been seduced by society's emphasis on ideas. We have reduced theology to ideas about God. We esteem professors who can finely slice nuances of meaning but forget the power of the storyteller. The older I get, the less ideas seem to move me. Yet I am still touched by stories, even those I have heard many times! Yesterday I put down a book I agreed with 100 percent because it never incarnated its truth in a story about real human beings. I recently went away from a sermon shaking my head because it illustrated ideas with more ideas, even though the ideas were good ones. My daughter panned it simply: "Too boring, nothing to connect to daily life," she said.

There is something powerful about a story. Yet how often small-church leaders will revert to ideas to persuade. Abstract, impersonal, disembodied thoughts, no matter how true they may be, won't move small-church people like a good story will. A story about their past, their heritage, their hopes, their dreams, their characters, their faithfulness, their lessons learned, their glory days, their lean years, their courageous decisions. There is power in stories to motivate.

Effective small-church leaders can use stories to achieve the following outcomes:

1. *Help a congregation cope with change.* At Harbor Church we once took a whole evening to share about the fire that had destroyed one of our previous church buildings. In the course of the discussion a photograph

was circulated showing the ashes of the old building in the foreground. That was what captured most people's attention. Looking in the background, however, I saw the roof of the building that was to become our new sanctuary. It was as if, even in the midst of tragedy and grief, God had already provided a solution. People knew the events, but as I told the story contained in that photograph our congregation took renewed strength in God. If God had seen us through changes back then, would not the divine be with us in the changes we were now facing?

2. *Help a congregation reshape its identity and self-understanding.* There are times when a congregation needs to clarify its calling, make a shift in its direction, or undertake a major change in its purpose. For these times effective small-church leaders will have collected the stories of the congregation's formation and its periods of significant change. These can be garnered by listening during home visits, especially to the oldest members among whom is likely to be one or more oral historians. History programs or informal storytelling nights can also serve the purpose. Questions such as "When did we first start doing X?" or "How did Y come about?" usually elicit more information than "Why?" Yet it is the answer to "Why?" that we are usually after. It takes keen listening to discover the passion in remembered actions. But once it is discerned, fed back, and confirmed, the key to a brighter future is found. For we become the true children of our forebears, not so much when we do what they did but when we act from the same heart they had.

3. *Inspire faithfulness in difficult circumstances.* Come with me back to Block Island again. The year was 1776. The congregation had built a meeting house, organized as a Baptist church, and called its first pastor. This pastor thought the mainland less vulnerable to British men-of-war, however, and he departed. Into this leadership void emerged one Thomas Dodge. Deacon Dodge faithfully shepherded the flock until the war ended. Then he went to seminary, came back, and pastored for twenty more years. He is described walking along the shores of Fresh Pond, meditating, praying for his people, and mulling over his sermons. Coincidentally two hundred years later my family built a house abutting Fresh Pond. Whenever I faced trustee trouble or the congregation was going through a challenge, I conjured up the image of Deacon Dodge and gained the strength to persevere.

4. *Galvanize a response to a particular situation.* Have I told you the story of Brad and the chicken fat? To prepare for our annual chicken barbecue, I conned two septuagenarians into parboiling six

hundred half-chickens. Brad and Bob duly showed up at 7 A.M. and fired up the pots. Brad also brought an old tarp to throw down on the kitchen floor to catch any grease spatterings. Well, as it turned out the tarp had a few holes in it. And chicken doesn't stop cooking just because it is out of the pot. Nor does it stop oozing. At 3 P.M., exhausted, Brad and Bob went to clean up and found that a half-inch of chicken fat had seeped under the tarp. For months our church had the shiniest kitchen floor on the entire eastern seaboard! Brad retold this story a number of times for different purposes, depending on the situation. To me he reiterated it so that I would do a better job in recruiting! "Get younger people!" he bellowed. I got the point. To others he told the story to entice them to have an equal amount of fun working for the Lord.

   5. *Empower individuals and release congregational faithfulness.* Heroes, elders, founder, matriarchs, and patriarchs of old are the stuff of legend in every small church. But they needn't be relegated to past history. Storytelling can bring them into the present to inspire a better future. Of course, in order to tell the appropriate story, it helps to know the stories, and to know the people, and to hear God's call.

CREATE A CLIMATE OF THE POSSIBLE

I have heard that it is impossible, aerodynamically, for the bumblebee to fly. It is a good thing no one told the bumblebee! Small churches, however, have been told many times and in many ways that they can't fly. Certainly God can work a miracle through a small church just as readily as through a large church. God can, but we don't believe it, so we don't let it happen. Good things can happen in our small churches, but usually one at a time. So even when we celebrate it sounds like a dirge. So little. So late. So what?

   Our society is prejudiced against smallness and we in the small church have internalized that value. Often our own denomination is prejudiced against small (read: troubled, dysfunctional, subsidized, dependent, and so on) churches, and we have internalized that assessment. It is an uphill battle to reclaim our rightful place in God's valuation. But it is a struggle we must engage in. For who ever won a battle they didn't show up for?

   Small churches can increase their self-esteem. And good leadership will be continually engaged in this enterprise. Effective small-church leaders will always do two things: pose the possible and celebrate the progress.

"Baby steps," one church consultant advocates, "help them take baby steps until they can walk again." Small victories are preferable to large paralyses! What is doable in the direction that God has called us? Let's do it! And when we finish let's pat ourselves on the back, praising God.

One of my churches has less than twenty attending each Sunday. Its newest member lives fairly close by, but for years he didn't realize the church was there! How could they make themselves more visible? parishioners asked. They were too introverted to knock on doors, too poor to buy advertising, too timid to try anything bold. Finally they figured out what they could do. They could produce a brochure of the history of the church. They could buy a case of Bibles from the Bible society. They could hold a yard sale on the church lawn. So they did. When I last visited them I was greeted with an excellent brochure, a big smile, and a half-emptied box of Bibles! And they had a great time doing it. Maybe not a big deal to you, but a huge confidence boost for them. When one of the members later called me to say that he was feeling God's tug to further ministry, I knew that possibility thinking had started to replace impossibility thinking.

Another church was almost ready to close its doors twenty years ago. Its members had a fateful decision to make. Into their sleepy, introverted, no-risk existence came a group of folk emotionally battered from another congregational setting. The members chose to make their church a welcoming, safe place for these refugees. They chose to embrace them and to work together to find a common future, even if it meant deviating from their sacred past. They found significance in loving the new folk. Eventually they became one group, more open to new possibilities than either was originally. Step by step they parlayed this new climate of congregational potency into real ministry and progress. They opened up a Christian daycare center. They produced a Christian rock concert series. They completed a $250,000 addition. They commissioned one of their members to minister in a sister church. They sent a group to install windows in a house that a Native American congregation was restoring. They simply would not, and will not, believe that they are "too small" a church. The climate of the possible is too strong.

RESHAPE THE REPERTORY

Even the most primitive tribe has a vast reservoir of behaviors. For small churches I call this behavioral reservoir a "repertory." This repertory is the stuff of small-church life. "The way we do things around here is who we are." Things are not relearned and redesigned willy-nilly. Small churches work out of habit. Small churches are comfortable and familiar with their habitual repertoire. Teaching new behaviors is difficult and ofttimes unnecessary. Often all that is needed is a reshaping or reapplication of existing behavioral patterns. Cloning and kaleidescoping are two ways that the existing repertory can be reshaped for further ministry.

"Cloning" means doing something that is very similar to something we already do. I remember an episode at Harbor Church. Our Sunday School superintendent wanted to connect with the parents of the Sunday School kids, especially the ones who seldom worshiped with us. How to do this? She knew very well that covered-dish suppers were a regular activity in our congregation. We loved them and could do one at the drop of a hat. No matter how many we'd had in the last month, someone always asked, "Why don't we have more covered-dish suppers?" So the superintendent scheduled a supper, asked all the regulars to bring a little extra, and then invited all the town parents who didn't attend another church to a Sunday School dinner. A number of new parents came. Before dessert the superintendent spoke about the plan and hopes for their children that Sunday School season. It was a positive, personal event. We used an old, faithful fellowship tool to start a new venture into evangelism. A cloned behavior allowed us to take a new step.

"Kaleidescoping" describes the forming of familiar elements into a new pattern. A Methodist congregation in Vermont was used to putting on monthly fund-raising dinners. It was also used to leading a worship service in a seniors residence. Then parishioners discovered that when the seniors had to cook for themselves their meals were not always healthy. So church members who worked at the supper took to making up plates of leftovers and running them up to the residence the next day. In the process a whole new ministry developed.

Some people are exhilarated by doing new and radical things. Most small-church people, though, are enervated by the mere thought of it. It is much more productive to utilize existing behavioral patterns in the shaping of new activities. Every congregation this side of God's kingdom needs to learn certain new behaviors and ways of being. Effective small-church leaders will save the energy and political coin required for truly necessary changes, and in the meantime use the congregation's own repertory to do viable ministry.

MODEL AND MENTOR

There are many ways to learn. Nowadays we bunch people in large groups, talk at them for an hour, and expect them to pick up what they missed by reading. But it was not always so. For thousands of years people learned by observing others doing, by doing themselves, and by getting feedback on how they were doing. Today we call this the "apprenticeship model," which is distinct from the academic model. The apprenticeship model has its advocates, but it is clearly the also-ran in today's educational world, including seminaries. So many leaders in our small churches, particularly pastoral leaders, try to introduce changes using the model that is most familiar to them instead of using the model that is most powerful in the lives of those on the receiving end!

Apprenticeship is a powerful vehicle. I doubt I could tell you two ideas I learned in seminary (important as they are), but I could write another book on the pastoral competence and confidence I gained working under the mentorship of Rev. Donald Crosby. Don strove to make worship an exciting and powerful experience, and he refused to be satisfied with my lapses into routine. Don lived out his belief in personal wholeness and helped me "get it." Don knew "when to hold 'em and when to fold 'em" and so helped this idealistic visionary to gain a modicum of political savvy. My two-year apprenticeship with Don was a period of my life filled with significant growth. Yet I did not immediately transfer its implications into small-church life.

Effective small-church leaders would do well to find out who in their church knows how to work its relational, communication, power, and meaning systems, and then apprentice with those persons. How do they think? How do they act? When do they act? Whom do they connect with about difficult matters? All of this and more can be learned the hard way or the easy way. Apprenticeship is the easy way. Believe me, I know about the hard way!

Effective small-church leaders would also do well to find apprentices, sharing our own expertise and inviting others to share their knowledge with those parishioners who want to grow in spirit and improve their competence in ministry and leadership. By observing and doing together, by affirming and critiquing, by mentoring and modeling leadership, people will learn and grow and become disciples, not simply of the mentor but ultimately of Jesus Christ.

LEARN THE LESSON

Let me contrast three approaches to a major disruption in the stability of life. In the business world, as we are experiencing it in these hectic early days of the twenty-first century, there is precious little stability. All is disruption, at least in the sense that the target is constantly in motion. An achieved goal today is simply the benchmark for tomorrow. Change is constant. A crisis is simply a big change, more of the same.

In the tribal world a crisis is a major deviation from the ways things were. Homeostasis has been disturbed and much energy is expended to survive the trauma and return to the "good old days." Although a crisis may in fact change the tribe's rituals, behaviors, and self-image, it happens as a by-product of survival.

In the small-church world, I believe, there are three possible outcomes to a crisis situation: (1) the crisis has hurts us, we are not as strong as we were before, we are lucky to have weathered it at all, but we are still alive; (2) the crisis really shook us but we outlasted it, life has returned to normal, we survived it; (3) the crisis was painful but served as a wakeup call, it taught us some things we needed to learn but didn't want to, ultimately it blessed us, we grew because of it. In effect, small-church leaders "construct" a congregation's response to the crisis. Wise leaders will find learning in the crisis and help the congregation to be stronger without denying the pain. Mediocre leaders will help the congregation survive, but without explicating the spiritual lesson inherent in the trauma, the congregation will be no stronger for the experience. Poor leaders will fall into the pain and not build anything productive out of the crisis, rendering the congregation weaker for the experience.

One of my congregations was recently hit by a major financial crisis. A buried, out-of-use fuel oil tank had sprung a leak. The church was obligated by state law to remove the tank and clean up the surrounding earth. It was an expensive proposition and provoked great anxiety since the final cost depended on the extent of the contamination. As the project got underway there was much anger and frustration, complaining and conflict. Yet through it all some significant learnings began to surface.

First, a member who had recently joined the church volunteered to oversee the project. Newly retired from the state's environmental watchdog agency, he was familiar with the forms and requirements and procedures to finalize this type of work. In time the congregation came to see his role as orchestrated by the Spirit. Second, when a subgroup of the church tried to sneak a financing method through at a business meeting called in regard to another matter, the church as a whole said, "No, we don't want to operate that way." Another meeting was subsequently called to put everything on the table. Attendees saw this crisis as an opportunity to address some of the unhealthy communication and control patterns that had emerged. And when the denomination came through with a multi-thousand-dollar grant to help offset the cost, church members no longer felt that they were alone. They saw their brothers and sisters in Christ coming to stand beside them in their time of need. This offered a big boost to their self-esteem. The financial dimensions of the crisis are still sobering, but spiritually the congregation has chosen to learn and grow, and they have.

SUMMARY

Let us review these six action strategies.

1. *Be a catalyst, not a champion.* The leader who makes every issue a personal crusade in a small congregation will soon resemble a voice crying in the wilderness. It is more effective to give support and encouragement to a like-minded member who is willing to lead the charge.

2. *Tell a tale.* Rightly used narratives have a tremendous power to motivate. Effective small church leaders will use stories to help a congregation cope with change or reshape its identity, inspire faithfulness in difficult circumstances, galvanize a response to a particular situation, empower individuals, and release congregational faithfulness. The best of ideas will have a greater impact when clothed in a story.

3. *Create a climate of the possible.* In contemporary society everything small is devalued. Small churches almost without exception have come to believe that they are inferior and impotent. Effective small church leaders will counter this attitude by posing the possible: inviting the small church to do something within their ability and confidence level. And then the effective small church leader will celebrate with the congregation their accomplishment. This process builds self-esteem and expands the activities that are possible.

4. *Reshape the repertory.* Small churches work out of their reservoir of learned and comfortable behaviors. New ministries can often be shaped from existing behavioral patterns. Cloning is the process of taking an exist-

ing activity, changing it in minor ways, and thereby bringing a new ministry into being. Kaleidescoping combines various familiar activities into a new behavioral pattern.

5. *Model and mentor.* Apprenticeship is a tried and true method of learning and change in tribal systems and in the small church. Yet it is not adequately employed in most of the small churches I know. Those who would be effective small-church leaders will both apprentice themselves to elders of the congregation and find those who are willing to learn at their own feet.

6. *Learn the lesson.* Every crisis in the life of a small church has the potential for learnings great enough to change the "way we do things around here." Effective small church leaders will utilize crises to move the congregation toward greater ministry, faithfulness, and fruitfulness.

I trust these strategies will prove helpful to small-church leaders. But how do we assess where to introduce movement toward greater health, faithfulness, and ministry in our small churches? This is the topic we turn to next.

CHAPTER ELEVEN

Small Churches Have a Future!

I enjoy reading the wisdom of today's church gurus. One of their current prognostications is this: by the year 2050, 75 to 80 percent of the churches existing today will be closed![1] I am assuming that they are not predicting the demise of the larger churches. But is this God's handwriting on the wall? Or is there hope for our smaller churches?

I remember predictions during my college days in the 1970s about the waning of marriage. What with free love, the breakdown of many traditional institutions, birth control, no-fault divorces, and a generation radically rethinking societal mores, marriage was definitely doomed. Subsequently I became a pastor and officiated at hundreds of weddings. To misquote Mark Twain, reports of marriage's death were premature. Marriage, albeit bruised, is still alive and relatively well now into the twenty-first century! Certain basic structures and relationships seem just plain necessary to humanity. In fact, the more society changes, the more people feel a need for these basic structures of life. Marriage is one such structure. I believe that the small (relationally based, single-cell) church is another.

Electronic religion, mega-churches, and a renewed interest in spiritual direction are all part of today's religious landscape. Who knows what additional forms and options will be a part of tomorrow's? Through it all, small churches will continue to provide the face-to-face experience of faith. Thousands of small churches will undoubtedly close in the decades ahead. But many new ones will be founded and many old ones will find new life.

One of the healthiest churches I work with is located in a small village east of Brockton, Massachusetts. It averaged eighty folk at the traditional service of worship. About two years ago parishioners felt the need to worship God in a style more natural for some of their younger members. They spent about a year preparing practically, psychologically, and politically.

Today total attendance is around 125! They offer three adult Bible studies, one called "Bible 101" for people who never heard of a testament. Upon hearing of a Native American church's start to remodel its worship space, a group went forth, cased the joint, order the needed materials, and have set up a schedule to install them. A few months ago one of the members was commissioned to go to a struggling church as an unpaid pastoral assistant to develop a ministry to college students. This congregation actively works to link members' gifts and passions with real opportunities for ministry. In the last few years this has resulted in a church preschool and a contemporary Christian band festival, to mention a few.

"What a great story, Tony," you might say. "That church has a rosy future, but what about the rest of us? We are not in such a place." Well, consider this. Fifteen years ago that same church was on the verge of closing. Attendance had shrunk to a few elderly, inflexible Yankee farmers. The town barely knew of the church's existence. It could not afford a full-time pastor. By every human standard that church was doomed. But we worship a God of resurrection. The church called a solid pastor with a vision. The old-timers set their minds to include and affirm new members as they joined. Tentatively they began to step out in faith. Slowly they began to blossom. How easy it would have been fifteen years ago to write them off. But God didn't. I believe God has a future in mind for each small church, even if we cannot yet see it.

I think of each of my small churches as a mission outpost in a needy world. Each one has the good news of new life in Jesus Christ. Each one is set in the context of thousands of souls with no vital connection to Christ's body. Each one has unlimited potential. Each one is small enough to relate personally to individuals and families outside the walls of the church. But, alas, many think themselves too small to be God's presence right here, right now!

Small churches have a bright future to the degree that each one coordinates with God's redemptive purpose. Our God is in the redemption business. Our God redeems lives from self-destruction to self-fulfillment. Our God redeems families from hurt and dysfunction to love and reconciliation. Our God redeems societies from sin and injustice to righteousness and health. And our God redeems small churches from despair and paralysis to joy and service.

Small churches become part of God's redemptive activity when they live out their divine calling. Small churches that have an infectious joy have a future. Joy is one of the primary gifts of the Holy Spirit. Not a happiness based on entertainment or even positive circumstances, but a fundamental delight to be alive, to be in fellowship, to serve other people, to be in God's family. It does not take visitors very long to sense whether they will be uplifted or depressed in a particular small church, and thus whether they will stick around. The small church that is a conduit for the joy of the Lord will be a blessing to real people.

My oldest church has been around for more than three hundred years. In all that time it has fluctuated little in attendance, nor has it used assertive means of evangelism. It just seems to attract new people as it goes along its merry way, primarily because its way truly is a merry way! Parishioners are warm and upbeat. When I visited with them at the end of an eight-week drought, the worship leader explained to us that the liquid falling from the heavens was something called "rain." We all cheered God for it. I left singing in the rain. I left filled with joy. If we don't offer people joy, they won't much care what else we say we have.

Small churches that connect people with their God-given purpose will have a future. As I write this, there is an "epidemic of success" in society. Thirty-somethings are multimillionaires. People are retiring early with more disposable income than they had when they worked! A lot of people have "arrived," only they don't know where. Fending off starvation, providing for one's family, and making money gives purpose to our existence until it is achieved. Then what? Is this all there is? The soul's emptiness becomes painfully exposed. One executive who grew a fledgling cable company into a media giant says that he still had to make the move from success to significance. Small congregations offer face-to-face relationships, hands-on mission, immediate opportunities for involvement, and a taste of the eternal. What better context to discern, develop, and deploy one's spiritual gifts than in the nurturing and accepting fellowship of a small church? What better place to cultivate, express, and embody one's passion than in a small church? What better place to find one's God-given purpose?

Small churches that care have a future. The personal nature of the small church is its divine gift to humanity. In the small church each person is important, each person can make a difference to someone else, each person can experience unconditional love, each person is called to live up to his or her potential, each person is of infinite worth. The people-centered quality of small-church life makes it necessary in each generation.

Small churches that distinguish the power of God from the vehicles of a previous day have a glorious future. These are churches that preserve the evangelistic zeal of their forebears as much as the sanctuary built as a result of that zeal. These are churches that praise God as naturally today as did those who donated the organ in their day. These are churches that would rather empower parishioners to address the needs of local people than to dole out dollars to distant charities.

Certain small churches have a future. Others do not. Those that can rediscover their joy, those that can reconnect people with their God-given purpose, those that can love others, those that can preserve the spirit of their heritage will have a glorious future. But those that fail to do so will wither away.

As for small-church leadership, both clergy and lay, three qualities will determine our future. First, small-church leaders must neither waste energy trying to recapture a once-glorious past nor think that it is possible to just maintain the status quo; nor should we attempt to use methods alien to the nature of the small church. Instead we must do our best to accept the small church unconditionally. We must love it as it is in order that it may become what God intends it to be. Second, we must familiarize ourselves, to the point of mastery, with the nature of the small church. I have attempted to outline the basic features of the small-church world in these pages. Here, as in any field, competence is required for successful navigation. Third, we must help our small churches to release the impulse of the Spirit that is often buried deep within. Truly blessed small-church leaders will help our flock to feel that each and every one of us is coming home as we move into God's tomorrow.

The challenge of quality leadership for the small church has never been greater. Society is moving at a rapid pace, and small churches are hard pressed to adapt. Churches are no longer esteemed. In our culture anything small is discounted, and often despised. Within small churches despair has all too often displaced joy, and a defensive stance of survival has all too often replaced a sense of potency and adventure. Yet small churches still have a central place in God's purpose. And God is still calling leaders to our small churches. Competent, caring, committed leaders are being raised up by the Spirit "for such a time as this." Leaders who love their people and invite them to be more lovable and loving. Leaders who love history and see it as something to build upon. Leaders who are spiritually secure enough to say, "Small is blessed." Leaders who see heaven reflected in the small congregation and therefore seek to polish the mirror. May you be such a leader!

CHAPTER 1

1. David Ray, "Growing and Caring as a Healthy Small Church" (Providence, R.I.: *The Five Stones*, 1989), audiocassette.

2. Lynn Wolcott, "Big Enough for 1400, but Too Small for One," *The Five Stones* 6, no. 4 (Fall 1988): 13.

CHAPTER 2

1. Paul S. Minear, *Images of the Church in the New Testament* (Philadelphia: Westminster Press, 1960).

2. Robert Redfield, "The Folk Society," *American Journal of Sociology* 52, no. 4 (January 1947): 293–303.

3. Harold Moore, "The Pastor as Family Therapist," *The Five Stones* 2 (Spring 1987).

4. Conversation with author.

5. Dolores Curran, *Traits of a Healthy Family* (San Francisco: Harper and Row, 1983), 23–24.

6. Carl S. Dudley, *Unique Dynamics of the Small Church* (Washington, D.C.: Alban Institute, 1977), 6.

7. Arlin J. Rothauge, *Sizing Up a Congregation* (New York: Seabury Professional Services, 1983).

8. Lyle E. Schaller, *Looking in the Mirror* (Nashville: Abingdon Press, 1984).

CHAPTER 4

1. Redfield, "Folk Society," 301.

CHAPTER 5

1. These steps were taken from my notes on a seminary course in church administration.

CHAPTER 6

1. Elenore Smith Bowen, *Return to Laughter* (New York: Harper and Row, 1954), 274–75.

CHAPTER 7

1. Elman R. Service, "The Ghosts of Our Ancestors," in *Primitive Worlds: People Lost in Time* (Washington, D.C.: National Geographic Society, 1973), 9–10.

2. Redfield, "Folk Society," 293.

3. Ibid., 298.

4. Ibid., 299–300.

5. Ibid., 300.

6. Ibid., 303.

7. Bowen, *Return to Laughter*, 74–75.

8. Ibid., 223.

CHAPTER 9

1. Jackson W. Carroll, ed., *Small Churches Are Beautiful* (San Francisco: Harper and Row, 1977).

2. Arthur Kinoy, *The Real Mystery of Block Island* (Block Island, R.I.: Block Island Historical Society, 1961).

3. David R. Ray, *Small Churches Are the Right Size* (New York: Pilgrim Press, 1982).

4. John A. Hostetler, *Amish Society*, 3d ed. (Baltimore: Johns Hopkins University Press, 1980), 285–86.

CHAPTER 11

1. Bill Easum, speaking to "Gathering of Church Champions" conference, the Leadership Network, Flower Mound, Texas (1999).

$\mathscr{W}$elcome to the work of Alban Institute...
the leading publisher and congregational
resource organization for clergy and laity today.

Your purchase of this book means you have an interest in the kinds of information, research, consulting, networking opportunities and educational seminars that Alban Institute produces and provides. We are a non-denominational, non-profit 25-year-old membership organization dedicated to providing practical and useful support to religious congregations and those who participate in and lead them.

Alban is acknowledged as a pioneer in learning and teaching on *Conflict Management *Faith and Money *Congregational Growth and Change *Leadership Development *Mission and Planning *Clergy Recruitment and Training *Clergy Support, Self-Care and Transition *Spirituality and Faith Development *Congregational Security.

Our membership is comprised of over 8,000 clergy, lay leaders, congregations and institutions who benefit from:
- ❖ 15% discount on hundreds of Alban books
- ❖ $50 per-course tuition discount on education seminars
- ❖ Subscription to *Congregations*, the Alban journal (a $30 value)
- ❖ Access to Alban research and (soon) the "Members-Only" archival section of our web site www.alban.org

For more information on Alban membership or to be added to our catalog mailing list, call 1-800-486-1318, ext.243 or return this form.

Name and Title: _____

Congregation/Organization: _____

Address: _____

City: _____ Tel.: _____

State: _____ Zip: _____ Email: _____

BKIN

The Alban Institute
Attn: Membership Dept.
7315 Wisconsin Avenue
Suite 1250 West
Bethesda, MD 20814-3211